CAMPFIRE STORIES

SCARY STORIES AND WEIRD ANIMAL FACTS TO SNORT, GASP AND SHIVER...

SLOW SPRINT

CONTENTS

CAMPFIRE STORIES

~ INTRODUCTION ~...2

~ WEIRD ANIMAL FACTS ~ 3

~ STORY TELLING TIPS ~...15

~ SPOOKY STORIES ~ 19

~ LEGENDS ~...30

~ SHORT STORIES ~..41

~ TRUE STORIES ~...74

CAMPING JOKE BOOK

~ INTRODUCTION ~...87

~ PUNS ~...88

~ SHORT JOKES~...97

~ LONG JOKES~ 129

~ RIDDLES ~ 149

~ FUNNY STORIES ~ 156

~ INTRODUCTION ~

SNORT, GASP, AND SHIVER

Camping should be fun. It's unlikely you'll be telling campfire stories every night on your trip. However, the night when the fire is flickering low could be your chance to make it the most memorable night of your camping getaway. But campfire stories are not always about scary and spooky tales. While a well told story can give everyone a shock, it's fun to laugh and simply have a great time.

That's why this book is separated into different parts. There are weird animal facts guaranteed to get a laugh and start a strange conversation. The spooky stories will give you the traditional campfire experience to scare the pants of your kids. Then there are the legendary stories every child should know about. And to finish, there are short stories so your kids can relax, roll up in a chair and entertain themselves at any time.

Enjoy the tales and facts in this book and I hope you create lasting memories on your next camping trip.

Bill Buck

~ WEIRD ANIMAL FACTS ~

GUARANTEED CONVERSATION STARTERS

Enjoy sitting around your campfire with a fun challenge about strange animal facts. Be sure to share this book around so others can get a turn at asking questions around. How many can you get right?

WEIRD ANIMAL FACTS

On average, how many spiders live in 1 acre of green area?
50,000

Can bats walk?
No. Their legs are so thin they cannot walk.

Can a kangaroo jump if you lift its tail off the ground?
No. They use their tail for balance.

What happens if you keep a Goldfish in a Dark Room?
It becomes pale and it will lose it color because the pigment production depends on light.

Who hunts more, the female or male lion?
The female hunts 90% of the time.

What animal runs faster? A Horse or an Ostrich?
Ostriches. They run 70 km/h, compared to 40-48 km/h for horses.

What was the world's smallest dog and how heavy it?
The world's smallest dog was a Yorkshire Terrier and it weighed just 4oz.

Can you drown a crocodile?
Yes. If you keep it underwater too long it will drown. Same with turtles, dolphins, wales and water snakes. Unlike fish, these animals require certain amount of air.

How many times can a song board sing in one day?
Up to 2000 times in one day.

What is one of the two non-human primates to have blue eyes?
Blue-eyed Lemurs

How many years can a Tarantula Spider survive without food?
More than 2 years.

How many ants are there for every one human on earth?
About one million ants per person.

Can cows sleep standing up?
Yes, they can.

Do cows dream while they're sleeping?
Yes, but only when they lie down flat. Cows don't dream when sleeping while standing.

What sentence contains all letters in the alphabet?
"The quick brown fox jumps over a lazy dog."

How long can an Alligator live?
Up to 100 years.

How heavy can a single Elephant's tooth weigh?
Up to 9 pounds for single tooth.

How do you escape from the grip of a crocodile's jaw?
Push your thumbs into its eyeball and it will let you go instantly.

How do you make a scorpion sting itself to death?
Drop a small amount of alcohol on it and it will go so crazy that it will sting itself to death.

What are the names for a male and female rabbits?
A male rabbit is called "bucks" and a female rabbit is called a "doe".

How do Flamingoes eat?
Flamingoes can only eat when its head is upside down.

Do ants ever sleep?
No. Ants never sleep. Also they don't breathe because they don't have lungs.

What do you call a group of owls?
A Parliament.

How much methane gas does a cow produce?
In a single day, a single cow can produce about 400 liters of methane gas.

How long and how heavy is a single Blue whale?
Blue whales weigh as much as thirty elephants and can be as long as three Greyhound buses.

How many lengths of its own body can a grasshopper leap?
20 lengths of its own body.

How big is a baby kangaroo at birth?
Only about an inch long — no bigger than a large water bug or a queen bee.

What is the farthest a human can detect a skunk's smell?
About a mile away.

Can a butterfly kill a cat?
Yes. In Uganda, Africa, there is a poisonous butterfly with enough venom to kill six cats.

How long have cats lived with humans?
For about 7,000 years.

How many muscles does a cat have in its ear?
There are 32 muscles in each cat ear.

Can Hippos run faster than humans?
Yes. Hippos can run 30 km/p on land.

How long does it take for a baby horse to walk and run after being born?
It usually takes less than an hour.

Do kangaroos live in trees?
Yes. There are eight different kinds of tree kangaroos in existence.

How many times per second can a woodpecker peck?
20 times per second.

How many lengths of its own height can a flea jump?
200 times its own height. This is equal to a man jumping the Empire State Building in New York.

What is heavier? The tongue of a blue whale or an elephant?
The tongue of a blue whale is about the same weight as a fully grown large elephant.

Do moths have stomachs?
No. Most moths do not eat at all. They usually consume liquid.

Can deer eat hay?
No. Deer doesn't have living bacteria to digest hay.

Can a skunk bite and throw it scent at the same time?
No. Skunks usually spray its bad smelling scent at predator. If that doesn't work, then it tends to bite the predator.

Can a snail grow new eyes?
Yes. If a snail's eye is cut off, it will grow a new one.

How many times on average does a cow poop?
16 times.

What is the most poisonous fish in the world?
The stonefish.

What animal was first domesticated by humans?
Goats. They were one of the first animal domesticated by humans about 10,000 years ago.

Where do dogs have their sweat glands?
A dogs sweat glands are in between their paws. Because they can only produce sweat on areas not covers with fur.

What do you call the fear of animals?
Fear of animals is called "Zoophobia".

What percentage of DNA is shared between a human and a slug?
Humans and slugs share about 70%.

What percentage of DNA is shared between a human and a chimp?
Human share 98.4% of our DNA with a chimp.

Can two tigers have the same stripes?
No. Two tigers never have the same stripes. The stripes are like fingerprints to them.

What's the longest ever recorded life span of a slug?
1 year, 6 months.

How many times does a whale's heart beat in a minute?
9 times a minute.

How many mice can a python eat in 6 months?
A python can eat 150 mice in 6 months. It can also swallow a whole rabbit whole.

How big and heavy does a panda weigh at birth?
A panda weighs 4 oz. at birth. It's smaller than a mouse.

How many times does a hummingbird's wings beat per second?
60 to 80 times per second.

What happens to a dolphin's brain when it sleeps?
Only half of a dolphin's brain sleeps at a time. The other half stays awake so the dolphin can come up for air when needed and prevent drowning.

If a chameleon is blind, can it still change to the color of its surroundings?
Yes, a completely blind chameleon will still take on the colors of its environment.

Do rodents' teeth stop growing?
No. A rodent's teeth never stop growing.

Is a hippopotamus born on land or in water?
Underwater. Hippopotami are born underwater.

How can you tell the gender of a turtle?
By the noise it makes. Males grunt and females hiss.

What do you call a group of goats?
A herd.

What color does a squirrel NOT see?
Red.

How many eggs does the average chicken lay each year?
260 eggs per year on average.

How long have sharks existed?
Sharks were around before dinosaurs.

How heavy was the largest squid ever found?
8,000 pounds

How many people die each from being stepped on by cows?
Approximately 100 people.

How many eyes does a butterfly have?
12,000 eyes! (that's a lot of eyes)

What is the loudest living creature?
Humpback whale.

What is the color of a hippo's sweat?
Pink.

Where can you find oysters that can climb in trees?
In the Caribbean.

How many feathers does a swan have?
Over 25,000 feathers.

What is considered the largest animal to have ever existed in the world?
Blue Whales

Do Giraffes have vocal cords?
No.

How many eyes does a starfish have?
Eight eyes. One at the end of each leg.

What insect regurgitates its food and then eats it again?
A housefly.

How long can a mole dig just one night?
300 feet.

What animal can see their 4 legs all the time, because of their eye placement?
Donkey.

What animal can change its gender to find better mating opportunities?
The oyster.

Where does the French Poodle originate?
Germany.

Do elephants drink water through their trunks?
No. They only suck the water part of the way up and then use their trunks to squirt the water into their mouths.

Does goat have teeth in their upper front jaw?
No.

How far can a Tuna Fish swim in a single day?
40 miles.

What animal has hair on its eyes?
The bumblebee.

How far out of the water can Penguin jump?
6 feet.

How many pounds can a baby whale gain in a day?
200 pounds per day.

How many vocal sounds can a cat and a dog produce?
Cats can produce over 100 vocal sounds, compared to 10 vocal sounds of a dog.

How long is a Cheetah's lifespan in the wild?
Up to 12 years

What animal's cornea can be used in human eye transplants.
Shark corneas.

What kind of skeleton does a butterfly have?
An exoskeleton. (skeleton on the outside)

What do you call the fear of spiders?
Arachnophobia.

What is the largest land predator?
Polar Bears.

How does Hippos attract mates?
By urinating and defecating (peeing and pooing).

What colors can butterflies see?
Red, green and yellow.

How many species of butterflies are there?
Approximately 24,000 species.

Do dogs see better in lots of light or a small amount of light?
Small amount of light. (When it's darker).

How far away can an elephant smell water?
Up to 3 Miles away.

How far away is it possible to hear an adult lions roar?
It can be heard up to 5 miles away.

How many goats are there on the planet?
Approximately 450 million.

What is the color of a Dalmatian at birth?
Completely white.

Do the teeth of a beaver ever stop growing?
No. They never stop growing.

What do you call fear of bees?
Apiphobia.

What animals have rectangle pupils?
Goats and octopus.

How many teeth does an African Elephants have?
4 teeth.

Do crocodiles eat stones?
Yes. All crocs swallow stones sometimes to help in digestion and add weight so that it can stay underwater.

Can horses vomit?
No.

What do you call a group of frogs?
Army.

Do starfish die of old age?
No.

What do you call a group of whales?
Pod.

Can a full-grown bear can run as fast as a horse?
Yes. A full-grown bear can run at speed about 40 km/h.

Why do frogs need to blink while swallowing?
Frogs can't swallow without blinking because they use their eyes to help push food into their stomachs.

What places on earth have no ants?
Iceland, Greenland, and Antarctica.

What animal eats their twin brothers and sisters before even born?
Sand Tiger sharks.

What animal is made of 98% water?
Jelly fish. They will evaporate if they stay in the sun.

What is the slowest moving fish?
The seahorse. It moves about 0.01 mph (0.016 km/h).

What animal is responsible for accidentally planting million trees?
Squirrels. Because they've buried nuts and forgotten where they were.

How far away can a great white shark detect blood?
Great white sharks can detect a drop of blood in 25 gallons of water and can even sense tiny amounts of blood from three miles away.

How long will a male emperor stand over a next waiting for a female penguin to get food?
Up to 2 months.

What is only animal on the planet where the male bears unborn young?
Seahorses.

What color skin does a polar bear have?
Black. (Underneath their fur)

What animal is born only male to then choose their sex to change to female?
Clownfish

How many voltages of electricity can an electric eel deliver?
600 volts, this can enough to knock a fully-grown horse.

How old was the longest-living tortoise lived?
152 years in the Galapagos Islands

How long does a Galapagos tortoises sleep?
16 hours a day and can go a year without food or water.

How far can a flying snake glide in the air?
Up to 330 feet and can even make turns in the air.

What animal has the longest pregnancy?
African elephants, for nearly two years long.

What animal can spend 12 hours and can consume 28 pounds of bamboo daily.
Panda.

How big is the largest squid on record?
59 feet long, and the creature's eyes are as big as beach balls.

How many ants can an Anteaters eat in day?
35,000 ants a day.

What kind of bat is responsible for drinking the blood of 25 cows every year?
Vampire bats.

How long will it take for a baby giraffe to stand after birth?
About 30 mins.

What animal sleeps up to 20 hours a day and is so sedentary algae grows on its back?
The three-toed Sloth

How many pounds of meat can a wolf consume in one sitting?
20 pounds.

How far and how long can an Ostrich cover in a single stride?
16 feet, and can reach up to 43 miles per hour.

What fish can reach 37 miles per hour and glide up to 655 feet, that is equivalent to more than the length of two football fields.
Flying fish!

What kind of animal spit out some of their internal organs via their anus as a defense mechanism?
Sea Cucumber.

What snake possess enough venom to kill an elephant?
The King Cobra.

How high can a king cobra stand up from the ground?
Higher than an adult human.

How large was the biggest bald eagles nest?
20 feet and weighed two tons.

What Australian animal is often mistaken as bear and can sleep 18 hours a day?
Koalas. These animals are marsupials not bears.

~ STORY TELLING TIPS ~
MEMORIES TO LAST A LIFETIME

SHOW DON'T TELL

The better the story teller, the better the kids experience camping and listening to stories. So it's important to work on your skills to deliver with impact. Kids love a good camping story. Scare them or make them laugh and it will be a very memorable trip. But if you're a monotone speaker and deliver a story that way, it'll be boring for everyone. The key is conversational narrations. Anyone can be a good story teller. Here are some golden rules to help you make your camping adventure simply awesome.

First timers

If you have never told a story before, then the starting point is to rehearse it to yourself. (Don't rehearse to the kids if you want them surprised or shocked...)

But don't just read it, like a recital. Act it out. Use conversational tones and deliver emphasis on the key story elements.

When you're actually telling the story, make sure your audience is in front of you. Sounds basic, I know, but you don't want them sitting beside you. This will make sure it is more impactful and you get everyone's attention.

Make sure the music is off and there are no distractions around. A silent night with fire crackling is the perfect opportunity. Before dinner or early afternoon is not advised because your campsite will be too busy. Also if there are other campsites around, make sure you're away enough to not get distracted by them.

The best environment is at night, the sun has gone or is going down, with a flames flickering from the fire, and everyone is fed. Don't have a big bonfire, because that will steal attention from your story.

If you are using a flashlight, make sure you hide it from kids. Otherwise they will be clicking the buttons and playing with it distracting from your story. Put them aside or temporarily out of reach while your delivering your story.

Pick the right story for your audience

It might seem obvious, but don't make the mistake of telling a deathly horror story to young kids who will have nightmares for the remainder of your camping trip. Make sure your story is age appropriate. You'll know by reading through it first.

As a story teller, you're basically a performer. Exaggerating the highs and lows so you can make everyone get hooked into your story. You may want to use props if they're relevant and will make your story better.

Don't make the mistake of thinking your story has to be really loud all the time. The greatest story tellers can speak soft and have their audience lean in with captured attention. This is the perfect setup for a loud shock on your main point or scare tactic.

The most effective stories have direct relevance to the immediate surroundings. If you're in the wilderness, then stories of wilderness makes sense. If you're telling a story about a ghost in a city building, it won't really have a big impact while around your campfire.

This doesn't mean you have to throw away your favorite story. You can simply adapt the story line to the surroundings. Switch out the city for the woods and the ghost is now among the trees. Maybe even in the exact forest you're camping in. Only 100 meters away...

An example of line modification is:
"the reflection of her face in the water was screaming"
to
"her 8-year-old face was screaming in the water reflection of the Yellowstone lake only 500 yards from here. "

Get creative, but still make it real. Body language and audience participation really helps your delivery. Get excited in the happy moments, get slow and low in the scary moments. Arm and body gestures will really help. Demonstrate how big something is or act out the motion if you're talking about walking or jumping. Using rhetorical questions with your audience will really get them engaged. For example:
"have any of you ever heard about the crocodile in Yellowstone lake?" with or without waiting for an answer, "let me tell you about it."

The best audience positioning

Surroundings and audience seating is very important. Especially if someone is working with you who will sneak up without being seen or heard.

The darkest part of the campsite should be behind the story teller. If you're entire campsite is dark, then it isn't an issue. But with a lot of modern campsites using installed lights, you might have to improvise or wait until it's dark enough. This really comes down to controlling distractions so you can confidently tell your story and leave a lasting impression.

Using props

Keep it simple. Shovels, sticks, bottles a tin can, they can all help the story if relevant. You don't have to make elaborate props at home and then bring them. If you want to prepare like a pro make sure you bring some bailing twine to setup secret devices in the woods to make sounds or create attention. It might take you 15 minutes to setup, but the impact of a well-timed 'booby trap' will create a great impact with your audience.

~ SPOOKY STORIES ~

SCARE THE PANTS OFF YOUR KIDS

Enjoy a mix of these classics and modern spooky stories around your campfire. For the most fun, be sure to read the tips on how to tell a campfire story. These are added occasionally in italics.

THE SKELETON LADY

This story begins not too long ago and not far away. Just to the north of here there is a country where it is winter for 7 long moths of the year. Now this particular winter had gone on much longer than usual and the people were beginning to run out of food and firewood. Inside one small house right out in the barren snow lands an old lady was beginning to get anxious.

(Now you have to put on old lady and old man voices, get anxious and rub your hands a lot as if cold).

"Oh, my husband I am so cold and hungry. Look at me my hands are blue! I am going to die I am sure of it."

"Don't worry my darling, winter will be over soon, we will have food again"

But the old lady looked very ill and continued to get anxious. Eventually the old man agreed.

"Very well my darling I will go and search for food. But before I go you must promise me one thing. You must not use the last two logs we have for the fire, we will need them to cook the food on when I return"

"Okay, okay I agree just go, please find food"

With that the old man went out in search of food. Time passed and the old man did not return, the fire was beginning to get lower and lower.

"Where is he? I'm hungry! I'm freezing! I am sure I will die" *(rub hands a lot)* Then the old lady had an idea.

"If I put just one of the logs on the fire he will be back soon and then we will still have one to cook the food with. Yes, yes that's what I'll do."

The old lady picked up one log and placed it on the fire.

"Oh that's much better, I'm so warm, he'll be back with food soon".

The old lady forgot how hungry she was as she sat close to the warm fire. But more time passed and still her husband did not return. It was beginning to get dusk outside and again the fire was getting lower and lower.

"Where is he? He must have found food and eaten it. I am going to be left here to freeze!" *(Lots of rubbing and groaning)*

Then the old lady had another idea.

"He must be back soon. If I put the last log on the fire it will be hot and ready to cook on when he returns".

With that the old lady put the last log on the fire. *(Make whooshing sound and cries of happiness)* But more time passed and the old man was not back. The last log began to burn lower and lower until all that was left was a tiny flicker.

The old lady got closer and closer to the fire. Then suddenly "Ouch" she burnt herself on it and began to bleed. She placed the finger in her mouth to lick it. *(make this action)*

"MMMMh this tastes good."

Then the old lady began to chew *(make chewing action up hand)*.

"Mmmm so good."

And chew, up her arm, and around her body *(act all this out - lots of chewing and mmhhing noises)* until all that was left was a skeleton.

"Mmhh that was so good, I feel much better but I'm still hungry."

Just at that moment she heard a rustling outside and the door opened. In came her husband with 2 rabbits in his hand.

"Look my wife I found foooo-----"

The old lady ran towards him and grabbed the rabbits.

"Mmmh these are good. MMhh MMhh" *(mime chewing rabbits)* "My husband I've just realized how meaty you are. Come here I want to eat you. I want Meat!"

With that the old man burst out the door and ran into the frozen wastelands as fast as he could. Behind him the old lady was running.
"I want meat, I'm going to eat you."

Luckily the old man could run fast and began to escape his wife. He ran further and further into the snow. In the distance was the sound of the old lady.

"I want meat. I'm going to eat you!" *(Each time you do this grab the arm of a member of the audience and fake chew it - you should be on your feet all the time now and miming the running actions.)*

Suddenly the old man came to the edge of a huge gorge that went as far as he could see that way *(look)* and as far as he could see that way *(look)*. There was no way across and coming closer was the sound of the old lady.

"I want meat. I'm going to eat you" (attack audience again)

Then the old man noticed a small wooden cottage. He ran to it and banged on the door. The door opened on a chain and a woman could be seen inside.

"Yes. How can I help you?"

"It's my wife. She's gone crazy she's going to eat me" *(act very panicked)*

"Very well I will help you but first you must bring me a bucket of water."

"What, she's going to eat me and you want water?"

"Yes"

"Okay, okay"

The old man searched around and found a bucket to get some water from the well. He took it to the woman who pulled out a ladle from her pocket and dipped it into the water.

"AAhh yes. Very good. Now I will help you"

In the distance the sound of the skeleton lady was very close
"I want meat. I'm going to eat you!" (attack audience)

The woman stood on the edge of the gorge and stamped her feet into the ground. Then she reached out and *stretched (say this word long and slowly as you stretch out)* to the other side and grabbed onto a tree. "Now you may cross."

The old man walked carefully across the lady's back *(mime this)* and reached the other side. Then the woman let go and PING went right back to the other side. She returned to her house.

Just then the skeleton lady arrived at the gorge.

"I will get you my husband. I will eat you. I want Meat!"

She banged on the door of the house.

"Yes. Can I help you?"

"You are too skinny to eat. You will help me cross the gorge."

"Very well I will help you but first you must bring me a drink of water."

"Help me now or I'll eat you anyway."

"Okay, Okay."

With that the woman stood on the side of the gorge and stamped her feet into the ground. She stretched across and grabbed onto the tree. The old woman began to run across.

"I want meat. I will eat you." When she was halfway across the woman let go and PING went back to the start.

"I want meaaaaaaaaaaaaaaaaaaaaaa....."
(Fade off and then crash to ground) CRASH the skeleton lady fell to ground and shattered to a million pieces.

(Say next part of story very slowly and quietly)

Now I said that I said that this happened not too long ago and not too far away. It is said that there is a little bit of magic in each piece of the skeleton lady's bone and that one day they will join together and come in search of..."MEAT" *(jump and attack audience then end)*

SOMETHING BLACK AND COLD

It started with little things, strange incidents that were sometimes inconvenient, sometimes almost amusing. But then the heavy trouble began... and the terror.

In the early 1970s, two sisters, Lois Dean and Diantha Summer, moved their families into two old houses in the middle of Rawlins, Wyoming, a small city in the Rocky Mountains. Lois and her husband and their six children moved into the big house. Diantha and her two sons took the carriage house right behind the main house.

Very soon, strange things began to happen in the big house. Lights kept turning on and off. At first the adults thought it was just the kids playing around. But they soon found that the lights seemed to be going on and off by themselves, even when no one else was around. Thinking it must be an electrical problem, Lois and her husband had the house rewired, but it kept happening.

When the children were playing games, they would leave the room for a minute and then come back to find game pieces missing. An older daughter found the colors in her makeup kits often smeared together. At first she thought the younger children were doing it, so she banished them from her room. But it kept happening even after she padlocked the door.

The family dog wagged his tail as though at an invisible guest, and his eyes followed something across the room. Sometimes, in the big house the bathroom cabinet would be found completely empty. Toothbrushes, combs and medicines would all be gone, to be found later in odd places. Again, Lois thought it was the children, but it even happened when they were all at school and she was alone in the house.

Then things began to get rough. A boyfriend of one of the girls was playfully climbing through a window. Something unseen picked him up and threw him inside, against a wall. That was the end of that boyfriend. He never came back for another visit.

Not long afterward, one of the younger boys said he had seen something in the garage. Mike, Diantha's 14-year old, decided to take a look. He started out the back door of the big house and suddenly felt two hands grab him and throw him through the air, back into the kitchen, into the refrigerator. He had red marks on his chest as if something had scratched him.

Lois was infuriated. She began yelling,

"I don't care who you are. I'm not putting up with you coming into my house and hurting kids!".

She was so angry that she was momentarily unafraid. She dashed out into the garage. There she saw a black shape.

"It was big and billowy," she says, "and it was dressed like a woman in something black and long."

It came toward her smoothly, as though it were on wheels...

"Something black and cold started coming out of it, like ribbons," she recalls. "It started wrapping me in those strands. I could feel their coldness. I couldn't move."

The she felt her sister, who saw the shape too, grab her from behind and jerk her away from the thing and back into the big house.

The sisters sat up all night, praying as hard as they could. The prayers may have had a good effect, for they never saw the thing again.

They took to calling that incident "the Main Event". Afterward, they felt the atmosphere to be a little less oppressive. However, everyone had a sense that the place was still not quite right, and before long, both families moved out.

In talking to the neighbors, only one event in the past seemed to hold a clue. Back in the early 1900s, a graveyard on the property was dug up and moved to another location. Rumor had it that two bodies were left behind. Were these two different restless spirits? We may never know.

WHITE EYES

The San Bernardino Mountains contain a lot of wilderness regions which saw substantial activity about 100 years ago. Here, miners and loggers worked to bring materials down to the Los Angeles basin. But, like most industries of that time, there was a high profit motive, and workers lives were not as important as they were now.

One day, a mine tunnel collapsed, trapping a number of men within. They were able to survive, after a fashion, by drinking water which seeped into the tunnels, eating rats, mushrooms, and their dead co-workers. They worked from within to dig themselves out, confident that on the other side, others were digging from the outside in. Well, maybe not that confident, since the mining company was not known for its compassion.

Well, it took them a while, but they finally managed to dig themselves out. Then, the formerly trapped miners found two surprises. First, since they had lived in darkness for a long period of time, they could no longer stand the sunlight, and their eyes were pure white---no color except for their pupils, which were dilated. Second, not one man had lifted a shovel to dig them out.

They then made a pact, these men, to take revenge on those who had abandoned them. Soon after, mysterious instances of men being killed in the mountains occurred. These men were usually found mauled, bloody and torn. Close examination showed the teeth marks on them were from human teeth. One man had been beat by his arm which had been torn off at the shoulder.

Soon thereafter, the mining company went out of business. No one was willing to work in those mountains, and even groups of men at night were at risk. Rumor had it that the White-Eyes were out for blood.

Now, since this happened about 100 years ago, and since only men were working in the mines, there should be no more White-Eyes around. So, we're safe---or are we? Several years ago, a hiker was found mauled on the trail, with human teeth marks.

TWIN POND GHOST

In 1972, when I was seventeen years old a friend had drowned in a pond on a farm. It is called the Twin Ponds because there are two ponds close together. He had been swimming with his cousins. His name was Gary and he was nineteen years old. He had natural curly shoulder length black hair. About one or two months after he had died his mother called me wanting me to come and stay with her for a while because she was alone. She lived in walking distance of the ponds in a small house that had four rooms downstairs and one room upstairs on a country road where there are not very many cars.

Gary's room was the one that was upstairs. The stairs were the type that had a wall on each side and a door at the bottom of the stairs. His mother told me that I could sleep in his room but I did not want too. Everything was still the same as he had left it. It still looked as if he would be back at any time so I stayed in a bedroom downstairs next to the stairs that lead to his bedroom.

One night when I had gone to sleep. I was either sleepwalking or dreaming, that I was walking down the road in the direction of the twin ponds. There was a bright full moon. As I was standing there wondering why I was walking alone on the road at night and where I was going, I saw someone walking up the road towards me from the ponds. As he got closer I saw that it was Gary, I tried to speak to him saying his name but he would not answer or look at me. He was walking at a slow pace, a few inches passed me with his head down and his eyes were half closed. I could have reach out and touched him but for some reason I did not. I saw that his hair was wet but it was not raining. Water was dripping off his hair and face and glistening in the moonlight. I watched him as he walked toward the house and disappeared. I guess he was going home.

What happened next is where it gets strange because I can swear that I was awake at this time. I woke up in bed thinking about the dream I just had when I got a funny feeling that I was being watched and that I was not alone. I turned over and looked at the open bedroom door. That is when I saw Gary standing there. He was leaning against the door with his arms crossed with a blank stare and smiling at me. He was wearing a white shirt with a V-neck, long baggy sleeves and dark pants, the same thing that he was wearing when I saw him on the road in my dream.

The curtains were open and the moonlight came through the window so I could see him clearly and everything in the room. I rose up on my elbow smiling back at him. As I started to speak to him, he started moving towards me. This is when I became scared and threw the blankets over my head because he was not moving in a normal way. He was floating and gliding with his arms down to his sides and I saw nothing below his knees. That was when I remembered that he was dead. I had forgotten until then. While I was under the blankets I started praying real fast waiting for the blankets to move or for him to touch me. After a few minutes that seemed like forever I peeped out from under the blankets and saw nothing so I jumped out of the bed and ran across the room and turned on the lights.

I must have made a lot of noise when my feet hit the hardwood floor and getting to the wall where the light switch was because his mother came running into the room from her bedroom with just her nightgown on and a worried look on her face asking me what was wrong. I lied and told her that there was nothing wrong. It was embarrassing for waking her up in the middle of the night and also I did not want to tell her that I thought I had seen her son's ghost. Then she started laughing and said
"You are lying!"
"You saw Gary didn't you".
"I know you did".
"I can tell by the way you are acting and the look on your face".
"You are real pale".
"He won't hurt you".
"I see him all the time". (That did not help any!)
I already knew he would not hurt me. That was not what scared me. I was not scared of him until I remembered that he was dead. We went back to bed and I slept with the light on the rest of the night. When it became daylight I told her that I wanted to go home but she wanted me to stay with her, telling me again that Gary would not hurt me.

As it was getting dark out the more nervous and scared I became. So she let me go home. I could not spend another night there. I still went and spent time with her during the day but I would not stay there at night. I would leave just before it started getting dark. She has died sense then and I know she is with her son now. It has been thirty years now and I still cannot go to the house at night.

THE BIG TOE

A boy was digging at the edge of the garden when he saw a big toe. He tried to pick it up, but it was stuck to something. So he gave it a good hard jerk, and it came off in his hand. Then he heard something groan and scamper away. The boy took the toe into the kitchen and showed it to his mother. "It looks nice and plump," she said.
"I'll put it in the soup, and we'll have it for supper."

That night his father carved the toe into three pieces, and they each had a piece. Then they did the dishes, and when it got dark they went to bed. The boy fell asleep almost at once. But in the middle of the night, a sound awakened him. It was something out in the street. It was a voice, and it was calling to him.

"Where is my to-o-o-o-e? " it groaned.

When the boy heard that, he got very scared. But he thought, "It doesn't know where I am, it will never find me." Then he heard the voice once more. Only now is was closer.

"Where is my to-o-o-o-e? " it groaned.

The boy pulled the blankets over his head and closed his eyes. I'll go to sleep," he thought. "When I wake up it will be gone." But soon he heard the back door open, and again he heard the voice.

"Where is my to-o-o-o-e? " it groaned.

Then the boy heard footsteps move through the kitchen into the dining room, into the living room, in the front hall. Then slowly they climbed the stairs. Closer and closer they came. Soon they were in the upstairs hall. Now they were outside his door.

"Where is my to-o-o-o-e? " the voice groaned.

His door opened. Shaking with fear, he listened as the footsteps slowly moved through the dark toward his bed. Then they stopped.
"Where is my to-o-o-o-e? " the voice groaned.
(At this point, pause. Then jump at the person next to you and shout)

YOU'VE GOT IT!

~ LEGENDS ~

FOLKLORE TALES FOR EVERYONE

THE GHOST

The train rumbled around him as he adjusted the throttle. The night shift was always the toughest, in the engineer's mind. He had rumbled through Timpa's a few minutes ago and was on his way to Thatcher. Not a bad stretch of road, and there was no better train in the entire Atchison, Topeka & Santa Fe Railroad.

He stretched a bit and yawned, trying to stay alert. And then he gasped. The lights had picked up the figure of a beautiful woman with long red-gold hair and wonderful blue eyes standing near the tracks. Too near! He sounded his horn to warn her away and then he realized that the light was shining right through her. She was a ghost!

She stepped into the center of the track, laughing and beautiful. She disappeared seconds before the train rushed through her. And then she was there, in the engine cab next to him. The scent of roses filled the air. He stared at the ghostly vision, bewitched by her beauty. With an enticing smile, she wrapped ghostly arms about his neck and kissed him. And was gone.

Dazed (and disappointed!), the engineer finished the run to Thatcher in a trance, completely forgetting to stop at the station. The fireman had to pour water on his head to snap him out of it.

The engineer decided not to tell anyone about the ghost, fearing for his job. But he was plagued by curiosity. Finally, he confided the story to a close friend who was a fellow engineer. To his surprise, the friend had heard about the ghost before. The ghost's appearance on the train was by no means uncommon. No one knew who the woman had been in life. But she always appeared on that stretch of track after dark, beckoning to the men on the railroad crew with a bewitching smile. Sometimes, said his friend, sometimes she would come right onto the train!

"Better not tell your wife about it," his friend advised.

The engineer never did.

THE KING OF SHARKS

One day, the King of Sharks saw a beautiful girl swimming near the shore. He immediately fell in love with the girl. Transforming himself into a handsome man, he dressed himself in the feathered cape of a chief and followed her to her village.

The villagers were thrilled by the visit of a foreign chief. They made a great luau, with feasting and games. The King of Sharks won every game, and the girl was delighted when he asked to marry her.

The King of Sharks lived happily with his bride in a house near a waterfall. The King of Sharks, in his human form, would swim daily in the pool of water beneath the falls. Sometimes he would stay underneath the water so long that his bride would grow frightened. But the King of Sharks reassured her, telling her that he was making a place at the bottom of the pool for their son.

Before the birth of the child, the King of Sharks returned to his people. He made his wife swear that she would always keep his feathered cape about the shoulders of their son. When the child was born, his mother saw a mark upon his back which looked like the mouth of a shark. It was then she realized who her husband had been.

The child's name was Nanave. As he grew towards manhood, Nanave would swim daily in the pool beside the house. Sometimes, his mother would gaze into the pool and see a shark swimming beneath the water.

Each morning, Nanave would stand beside the pool, the feathered cloak about his shoulders, and would ask the passing fishermen where they were going to fish that day. The fisherman always told the friendly youth where they intended to go. Then Nanave would dive into the pool and disappear for hours.

The fishermen soon noticed that they were catching fewer and fewer fish. The people of their village were growing hungry. The chief of the village called the people to the temple. "There is a bad god among us," the chief told the people. "He prevents our fishermen from catching fish. I will use my magic to find him." The chief laid out a bed of leaves. He instructed all the men and boys to walk among the leaves. A human's feet would bruise the tender leaves, but the feet of a god would leave no mark.

Nanave's mother was frightened. She knew her son was the child of a god, and he would be killed if the people discovered his identity. When it came turn for the youth to walk across the leaves, he ran fast, and slipped. A man caught at the feathered cape Nanave always wore to prevent him from being hurt. But the cape fell from the youth's shoulders, and all the people could see the shark's mouth upon his back.

The people chased Nanave out of the village, but he slipped away from them and dived into the pool. The people threw big rocks into the pool, filling it up. They thought they had killed Nanave. But his mother remembered that the King of Sharks had made a place for her son at the bottom of the pool, a passage that led to the ocean. Nanave had taken the form of a shark and had swam out to join his father, the King of Sharks, in the sea.

But since then, the fishermen have never told anyone where they go to fish, for fear the sharks will hear and chase the fish away.

THE BEAR LAKE MONSTER

If you travel to Bear Lake in Utah on a quiet day, you just might catch a glimpse of the Bear Lake Monster. The monster looks like a huge brown snake and is nearly 90 feet long. It has ears that stick out from the side of its skinny head and a mouth big enough to eat a man. According to some, it has small legs and it kind of scurries when it ventures out on land. But in the water - watch out! It can swim faster than a horse can gallop - makes a mile a minute on a good day. Sometimes the monster likes to sneak up on unwary swimmers and blow water at them. The ones it doesn't carry off to eat, that is.

A feller I heard about spotted the monster early one evening as he was walking along the lake. He tried to shoot it with his rifle. The man was a crack shot, but not one of his bullets touched that monster. It scared the heck out of him and he high tailed it home faster than you can say Jack Robinson. Left his rifle behind him and claimed the monster ate it.

Sometimes, when the monster has been quiet for a while, people start saying it is gone for good. Some folks even dredge up that old tale that says how Pecos Bill heard about the Bear Lake monster and bet some cowpokes that he could wrestle that monster until it said uncle. According to them folks, the fight lasted for days and created a hurricane around Bear Lake. Finally, Bill flung that there monster over his shoulder and it flew so far it went plumb around the world and landed in Loch Ness, where it lives to this day.

Course, we know better than that. The Bear Lake Monster is just hibernating-like. Keep your eyes open at dusk and maybe you'll see it come out to feed. Just be careful swimming in the lake, or you might be its next meal.

HOW THE BEAR LOST HIS TAIL

Long, long ago there were only creatures on the earth. There were birds, bears, deer, mice, everything but people. In this long ago time, all the animals spoke the same language. And just like some people nowadays, they played tricks on one another and made each other laugh. They also helped each other. So it was with all the animals.

One day in the winter when the lakes had frozen, but before the winter sleep, Bear was walking along the lakeshore. As he was walking, he came upon Otter sitting near a hole on the ice with a pile of fish.

"You've got a mighty big pile of fish there," Bear said. "How did you get them fish?"

Instead of telling how he dove down into the water and caught the fish, Otter decided to trick Bear. You see, back then Bear had a very long bushy tail. He was very proud of his tail, and all the animals knew it.

"The way I catch my fish is by putting my tail in this ice hole," Otter explained. "I wiggle it around once in a while so the fish see it. When a fish bites onto my tail, I quickly pull it up and out of the water."

"That sure is an easy way to catch fish," Bear said. "Do you mind if I use your fishing hole?"

Otter, laughing behind the Bear's back, said, "I have enough fish. Use my fishing hole as long as you like." Then Otter picked up his fish and walked away. Bear carefully poked his tail into the ice hole and waited. He waited and waited. Once in a while he'd wiggle his tail so the fish could see it. Bear waited until the sun began to set, but not one fish even nibbled at his tail. At last, he decided to go home, but when he tried to stand up, his tail had frozen into the ice! He couldn't move! He pulled and pulled at his tail, but it was stuck tight. Finally, he pulled with all of his strength and ripped off half his tail!

Now you know why the Bear has a short tail, and remember . . . don't always believe what people tell you.

LA LLORNNA

This is a story that the old ones have been telling to children for hundreds of years. It is a sad tale, but it lives strong in the memories of the people, and there are many who swear that it is true.

Long years ago in a humble little village there lived a fine looking girl named Maria Some say she was the most beautiful girl in the world! And because she was so beautiful, Maria thought she was better than everyone else.

As Maria grew older, her beauty increased and her pride in her beauty grew too When she was a young woman, she would not even look at the young men from her village. They weren't good enough for her! "When I marry," Maria would say, "I will marry the most handsome man in the world."

And then one day, into Maria's village rode a man who seemed to be just the one she had been talking about. He was a dashing young ranchero, the son of a wealthy rancher from the southern plains. He could ride like a Comanche! In fact, if he owned a horse, and it grew tame, he would give it away and go rope a wild horse from the plains. He thought it wasn't manly to ride a horse if it wasn't half wild.

He was handsome! And he could play the guitar and sing beautifully. Maria made up her mind-that was, the man for her! She knew just the tricks to win his attention.

If the ranchero spoke when they met on the pathway, she would turn her head away. When he came to her house in the evening to play his guitar and serenade her, she wouldn't even come to the window. She refused all his costly gifts. The young man fell for her tricks. "That haughty girl, Maria, Maria! " he said to himself. "I know I can win her heart. I swear I'll marry that girl."

And so everything turned out as Maria planned. Before long, she and the ranchero became engaged and soon they were married. At first, things were fine. They had two children and they seemed to be a happy family together. But after a few years, the ranchero went back to the wild life of the prairies. He would leave town and be gone for months at a time. And when he returned home, it was only to visit his children. He seemed to care nothing for the beautiful Maria. He even talked of setting Maria aside and marrying a woman of his own wealthy class. As proud as Maria was, of course she became very angry with the ranchero. She also began to feel anger toward her children, because he paid attention to them, but just ignored her.

One evening, as Maria was strolling with her two children on the shady pathway near the river, the ranchero came by in a carriage. An elegant lady sat on the seat beside him. He stopped and spoke to his children, but he didn't even look at Maria. He whipped the horses on up the street.

When she saw that, a terrible rage filled Maria, and it all turned against her children. And although it is sad to tell, the story says that in her anger Maria seized her two children and threw them into the river! But as they disappeared down the stream, she realized what she had done! She ran down the bank of the river, reaching out her arms to them. But they were long gone.

The next morning, a traveler brought word to the villagers that a beautiful woman lay dead on the bank of the river. That is where they found Maria, and they laid her to rest where she had fallen.

But the first night Maria was in the grave, the villagers heard the sound of crying down by the river. It was not the wind, it was La Llorona crying. "Where are my children?" And they saw a woman walking up and down the bank of the river, dressed in a long white robe, the way they had dressed Maria for burial. On many a dark night they saw her walk the river bank and cry for her children. And so they no longer spoke of her as Maria. They called her La Llorona, the weeping woman. And by that name she is known to this day. Children are warned not to go out in the dark, for, La Llorona might snatch them and never return them.

CREAK

"Creak", a sound, faint, distant, but still heard.
"Crack", something snapping, or being trampled on.

The man sits in his room, reading. The room is silent except for the quiet fire burning.
"Creak". Just the house settling, nothing more.
"Crack", Perhaps some small animals outdoors.
"Whoosh", Was that the wind?
The man stands up and peeks out the window. A clear night is all he sees, the full moon brilliant in the sky. Laughing at his nervousness, he returns to his book.

"Creak", the man now silently chuckles at the sound.
"Crack", how could he have been scared of some sounds.
"Whoosh", must be breezy out tonight.
"Thump"...did that come from within the house?
The man stares into the fire, trying to calm his jangled nerves.
"Creak"...
"Crack"...
"Whoosh"...will the sounds never cease?
"Thump"..."Thump"..."Thump"...

Closer, he thinks, the sounds are getting closer. He shuts the book and closes his eyes, and thinks of something besides his wild imagination.
"Creak"
"Thump"
"Crack"
"Thump"
"Whoosh"
"Thump"..."Thump"..."Thump"...a pause?
    The man moves quietly, slowly, towards the door with a nervous gait. "Thump"...a step back..."Thump"...yes, it's getting closer. "Thump"...he stares at the door, trying to somehow see through it..."Thump"...he reaches slowly for the doorknob, hand shaking, no longer able to take not knowing..."Creak", a loose floorboard, near the door outside..."Thump", he slowly opens the door...

    "A scream"
    ...silence...

LOOKING FOR TROUBLE

Once there was a family with a mom, a dad, and two brothers. Sometimes the brothers got along and sometimes they didn't, but when they wanted something from their parents, they ALWAYS worked together.

One week in the late summer, they decided what they wanted was to go camping at Goblin Creek that weekend. "Please please please dad?" they begged. "Pleeaaaaaaaaasseeeeeeee mom?" they whined.

Their parents told them that camping wasn't always as much fun as it sounded like. Sometimes it rained, and everything was too wet to play. Sometimes it got very cold at night, with only a tent around you.

short-campfire-ghost-stories-02; scary campfire story and at Goblin Creek, sometimes other things happened too.

"What KIND of things happen there?" the boys asked?

"Just believe us," said their father, "It's the sort of place where if you don't believe anything can happen, it probably will, just to prove you wrong."

"It's not the place to go looking for trouble," said their mother, "Or trouble will find you."

Going camping and not taking advantage of all the new ways to make trouble for each other did not sound like very much fun to the brothers, but they'd already used up the ways they could think of to get around all the boring rules at home, so they were not going to give up on camping yet.

All week long they asked to go camping that weekend at Goblin Creek. "Please please please dad?" they begged. "Pleeaaaaaaaaasseeeeeeee mom?" they whined. They kept begging, and they kept whining, and eventually their parents gave in.

The brothers were super excited, until it rained almost as soon as they arrived, the very first day. "Can't we play by the Creek?" they asked. "No, boys," said their father, "Everything is slippery, and you could fall in and get hurt or drown"

"Sorry, boys," said their mother, "Everything is muddy, you'll be complete

39

messes, and we don't have a way to do laundry out here." "UGH!" grumbled the older brother, " wish I was somewhere dry"

(At this point, pull on a hidden string that moves a stick through rusting leaves behind where your kids are sitting)

"Careful," said their father, "The goblin caves are dry, deep down under the ground where the rain doesn't go." "Oh whatever," replied the older brother, "I don't believe you."

After a day stuck sheltering from the rain under their parents' watchful eyes, the boys looked forward to having their own tent at night, where they could at least stay up late without their mom and dad knowing.

Once the sun set, though, it got very cold. They sat huddled and called out to their parents in their own tent next door. "Moooooom. Daaaaadd. It's COLD." "We warned you," called back their dad. "Just lie down with the sleeping bags closed around you," called back their mom, "If you go to sleep, you won't notice being cold until the sleeping bags warm up." "ARGH!" griped the younger brother, "I wish I were somewhere warm!"

(At this point, pull on another pre-hidden string, to make a tree branch creak)

"Careful" said their mother, "The goblin cook pots are plenty hot" "Yeah, right" replied the younger brother, "I don't believe in goblins."

The next morning, when their mom went to check on them, the brothers' tent was empty. "Oh no!" she wailed, "They must have gone looking for trouble..."

(At this point, since the real mother is probably telling this part of the story, the real father makes a horrible, bestial attack sort of sound, to cut her off)

~ SHORT STORIES ~

HUNKER DOWN FOR WILDERNESS READING TIME

After a big day of activities some kids want to rewind with a good story they can relax and use their imagination with. This collection of short stories is designed for that moment when they want to curl up in a chair and relax.

THE BROOMTOWN CURSE

There is an old legend about the history surrounding this campsite that says there was some Civil War fighting just a few miles down the road. And rumors that there used to be a little settlement hidden back in the deep woods - just on the other side of this camp. Of course back then -- we're talking over a hundred and fifty years ago -- that area would have been what you call deep woods, not just the backside of a campground like it is now.

Not many folks around here even remember there was another settlement, but when I was up here scouting out this campsite I did meet one old-timer that remembers. I never did get his name, everyone just called him "Pop." But he told me some of the history of this area. He even told me the legend about this little settlement. Said his grandfather told him about it. Claimed his grandpop used to hike into the woods where it was supposed to be, but all he ever found was some rotten logs and pieces of old black cast iron kettles.

Said its name was Haven, but back then everyone called it "Broom Town."

Now, according to Pop, it was around 1850 when this little settlement got started. Matter of fact, it was so long ago that the roads into it are all overgrown with trees and underbrush now - the forest just ate it up, and no mention of Haven or Broom Town shows on any map. But Pop said
the main road to it ran right through this campsite we're in now.

He's pretty sure he could guide us there, if we wanted, but he tells me that beside himself, there are few folks who even remember the settlement, much less where it was, or anything else about it.

Now back then -- remember, this was over a hundred and fifty years ago - when people picked a place for a settlement, they often picked it for defensive reasons, for protection. A lot of times they would even build log walls around it, almost like a fort. And this settlement had plenty reason to worry about protection. You see, all the folks who lived there had been suspected of witchcraft, of being witches and warlocks, and had fled their homes and villages to keep from being persecuted - or worse, burned at the stake.

That is the reason the settlement was so far off the beaten path, hidden away from the main roads and other towns. Like I said, its real name was

'Haven', but because of all the witches, I mean settlers, that lived there, everyone called it Broom Town. For hundreds of miles around people knew of Broom Town, but not exactly where it was.

In fact, they used to have some old sayings about how bad it was to be in Broom Town. Like if a fellow got in trouble with his wife, they'd say' "He better head to Broom Town", or if a young lady wasn't acting so lady-like they'd say; "If she's not careful she'll end up in Broom Town." Some parents even used Broom Town like a bogie man - they would tell their kids that if they were not good they would end up in Broom Town. Yep, Broom Town had quite a reputation, and mystique too. That means it was all mysterious and scary, and stuff.

In fact, many folks who knew about Broom Town thought that it was full of magic, and curses, and witch stuff, but of course we will never really know. It's gone now, and there isn't any written record of it anywhere. Except for the diary of course, but it didn't mention Broom Town
by name.

What we do know, however, is that not everyone who went looking for Broom Town found it, and those who did find it never talked about it. Like I said, there is no written record of life there,
but there is a written record... of death – in the dairy.

Didn't I tell you about the dairy?
Well, according to Pop, when they were building the new turnpike, some workers found an old leather-bound battle diary. Not far from here.

It seems that during the Civil War a troop of soldiers attacked and destroyed Broom Town, and killed everyone there. Now here's the weird thing, there is no record of which side did it. No one knows if it was the North or the South.

The dairy did have a name in it, a Captain's name, Captain John Bell. But the problem was that the name, Captain John Bell, was shared by two men. One was a captain for the South and one was a captain for the North. And both were in the area around that time. And both died around the same time too. No one could ever tell which one the battle diary belonged to. So all that we are left with is an entry in a battle diary.

This is what it said:
Saturday - While on reconnaissance discovered small fortified position in small valley. Unable to tell if friend or foe. From tall tree my spotter can see

people moving behind walls. The response to my questions shouted at the people behind the walls is one of rebuke. We are told to go away. In desperate need of food and supplies. Have determined activities suspicious and possibly hostile, will attack at dawn tomorrow. Will use last of dynamite to blow main gates.

Sunday Noon - Action successful. Battle was short, all fought against us but our training proved out in the end. 2 dead 3 wounded from unit, wounded able to move. Must move out soon. Men restless, superstitions running wild in unit. Many defenders yelled curses as they fought, and spoke in unknown language.

Sunday Night - Camp set up 1 mile south of previous position. Monday morning - Our position harassed by assassins, 2 dead, wailing and screams occur just before attack. Our cook claims must be banshees.

Tuesday morning - Harassed again over night, 4 dead. Am starting to believe in banshees. And that was the last entry in the book. Now that was a pretty interesting story, but what happens next is even more interesting. You see, the story of Broom Town had been forgotten until a fellow named Alfred Bell, and his brother Thomas, came visiting the area, somewhere around 1910.

You know that last town we passed coming into camp? Well, it used to be a frontier town around the time of Broom Town, and that's where the brothers stayed. They stayed in a hotel called the Manor House. It was a pretty fancy place for those times, and it's what happened in that fancy hotel that started the real legend of the Broom Town Curse.

What happened was, that on the very first night the Bell brothers stayed there, the other guests of the hotel were awakened in the middle of the night by a terrible commotion. They reported that in the wee hours of the morning, around 2:00 am, they heard wailing and screams coming from somewhere in the hotel. It lasted for about 20 minutes.

And during that time, the winds howled outside, (some said it sounded like demons howling), and the lights went out, and people even reported that the doors to their rooms shook real hard - like someone trying to get in.

By the time everything settled down, and someone thought to check the brother's rooms, hours had passed, but when they opened the door - both men were unquestionably dead. But no wounds could be found. The only blood came from where one brother had bitten his own tongue off, and it lay on the floor beside him.

Their faces were frozen in horror, eyes opened wide in shock, the pupils rolled back out of sight so that only the white of the eye could be seen. Their hands were raised in front of them as though they were trying to protect themselves, or ward off something.

Well, back then there were still people who remembered the Broom Town massacre, but they did not put two and two together until Alfred and Thomas's cousin came to get the bodies.

You see, his last name was Bell too, and the same thing happened to him. It was about 11:00 at night. Most of the hotel guests had already gone to bed, and Cousin Bell was one of them. In the room with him was a traveling salesman. They had met on the stage ride to town, and decided to share a room and split the cost. They flipped a coin for the bed, and the cousin lost.

So there he was, on the floor, sleeping on some quilts near the fireplace. According to the salesman, it was just about midnight when Cousin Bell started crying out in his sleep. This woke the salesman, and from the bed he watched as Cousin Bell tossed and turned.

He could see him fairly clearly in the glow from the coals of the fire. Suddenly Cousin Bell yelled and sat straight up. The salesman was about to say something when an awful screech sounded in the room. Outside the window, the winds rose to storm pitch, howling, like, well like banshees. And the shutters rocked on their hinges, banging against the windows.

The salesman said he was so scared he covered his head, and just peeked out from under the covers. He saw this huge black shadow in the center of the room. Cousin Bell had crawled to a corner, and was half standing half crouched, his back supported by two walls where they came together.

He was yelling NO!! NO!! and seemed to be trying to bat something away from his face with his hands, but the salesman couldn't see anything there. The shadow moved closer to the cousin, and as it did the salesman could see the other side of the shadow reflected in the dresser mirror.

It was horrible. It looked as though hundreds of heads hung attached to the big black shape of that shadow. There were adult heads, both young and old, there were the heads of children, boys and girls.

And, as the salesman watched one of the heads would open its mouth and wail, then the others would join in. Then the eyes would open, but there were no eyes -- just a hot red glow, much like the coals in the fireplace.

With all the eyes open, a reddish glow brightened the room, and in the mirror the salesman saw that some of the heads still had what looked like blood on them.

One head in particular had been split almost in half, and the brain oozed out it, all globbish and ugly. Several heads had only one eye, and one even had its nose cut off.

The salesman was afraid he was going to be sick, but he was more afraid of those screaming heads – so he just watched from under the covers, terrified, as that black shadow and those wailing heads loomed in the center of the room.

The heads wailed and screeched again, then moved closer to the corner where Cousin Bell was crouching in fear. He said he heard him yell and scream in terror, but he could not see him because the shadow covered him completely.

Then all of a sudden, everything got quiet. The screaming and screeching stopped. The wind stopped howling and the shutters stopped flapping. The salesman stayed hid under the blanket, and it was many minutes before he peeked out again. When he did, the shadow was gone, the wind had stopped, and Cousin Bell was dead in the corner of the room. Face frozen in horror, eyes rolled back – just like Alfred and Thomas. The salesman jumped from the bed, ran to the door, and flung it open - screaming.

Well, the story of the salesman traveled fast, and soon few people would come to the small town or stay at the hotel. Then one day, a few years later, an old woman showed up at the hotel. When people on the street asked her if she planned to stay there she replied, "Sure, I ain't related to them that be cursed." When asked what she meant, she told them the story of Broom Town. The real story. That is when they remembered the rumor of curses and so forth.

But, the old woman told them more than just rumors, she knew what really happened that day.

You see, when the massacre was over that day, after every one of the settlers was dead, the soldiers had time to look around, and what they saw scared them. Big iron cauldrons, (big black pots), on the fires, brooms leaning on every house step, and a black cape in almost every closet.

The soldiers became really afraid when they found out the people they just killed might have been witches. To solve the fears of his men, Captain Bell told them that if they cut off the heads of the witches and buried them separate from the bodies, then the dead souls of the witches could never find them, - - so that is what they did, to every last one of them.

Unfortunately for Captain Bell - and his relatives, he was wrong. Dead wrong.

Now, if anyone who took part in that raid, or even any of their relatives ever comes within 10 miles of Broom Town, the witches come to take their revenge. But, because the heads are not attached to the bodies, they can only move in the magic black shadow of the curse. And their angry headless spirits follow, separately, wildly, frantically trying to find their cut off heads, and that is what causes the sound of a howling wind and the screaming banshees.

Through the years, many people have been visited by the specter of that dark black shadow and those screaming wailing heads of the witches. In fact, part of the old legend says that is why both Captain John Bell's disappeared at the same time. They were related somehow, and the screaming banshees took their revenge on both of them, and their unsuspecting relatives. Of course that was a long time ago, and it may just be an old story somebody made up, but I hope there are no distance relatives of Captain Bell, or the other attackers, camping here tonight.

But… if the winds start to blow real hard, well…...

A WICKED WOMAN

It was because she had broken with Billy that Loretta had come visiting to Santa Clara. Billy could not understand. His sister had reported that he had walked the floor and cried all night. Loretta had not slept all night either, while she had wept most of the night. Daisy knew this, because it was in her arms that the weeping had been done. And Daisy's husband, Captain Kitt, knew, too. The tears of Loretta, and the comforting by Daisy, had lost him some sleep.

Now Captain Kitt did not like to lose sleep. Neither did he want Loretta to marry Billy--nor anybody else. It was Captain Kitt's belief that Daisy needed the help of her younger sister in the household. But he did not say this aloud. Instead, he always insisted that Loretta was too young to think of marriage. So it was Captain Kitt's idea that Loretta should be packed off on a visit to Mrs. Hemingway. There wouldn't be any Billy there.

Before Loretta had been at Santa Clara a week, she was convinced that Captain Kitt's idea was a good one. In the first place, though Billy wouldn't believe it, she did not want to marry Billy. And in the second place, though Captain Kitt wouldn't believe it, she did not want to leave Daisy. By the time Loretta had been at Santa Clara two weeks, she was absolutely certain that she did not want to marry Billy. But she was not so sure about not wanting to leave Daisy. Not that she loved Daisy less, but that she--had doubts.

The day of Loretta's arrival, a nebulous plan began shaping itself in Mrs. Hemingway's brain. The second day she remarked to Jack Hemingway, her husband, that Loretta was so innocent a young thing that were it not for her sweet guilelessness she would be positively stupid. In proof of which, Mrs. Hemingway told her husband several things that made him chuckle. By the third day Mrs. Hemingway's plan had taken recognizable form. Then it was that she composed a letter. On the envelope she wrote: "Mr. Edward Bashford, Athenian Club, San Francisco."

"Dear Ned," the letter began. She had once been violently loved by him for three weeks in her pre-marital days. But she had covenanted herself to Jack Hemingway, who had prior claims, and her heart as well; and Ned Bashford had philosophically not broken his heart over it. He merely added the experience to a large fund of similarly collected data out of which he manufactured philosophy. Artistically and temperamentally he was a Greek-- a tired Greek. He was fond of quoting from Nietzsche, in token that he, too, had passed through the long sickness that follows upon the ardent search

48

for truth; that he too had emerged, too experienced, too shrewd, too profound, ever again to be afflicted by the madness of youths in their love of truth. "'To worship appearance,'" he often quoted; "'to believe in forms, in tones, in words, in the whole Olympus of appearance!'" This particular excerpt he always concluded with, "'Those Greeks were superficial--OUT OF PROFUNDITY!'"

He was a fairly young Greek, jaded and worn. Women were faithless and unveracious, he held--at such times that he had relapses and descended to pessimism from his wonted high philosophical calm. He did not believe in the truth of women; but, faithful to his German master, he did not strip from them the airy gauzes that veiled their untruth. He was content to accept them as appearances and to make the best of it. He was superficial- -OUT OF PROFUNDITY.

"Jack says to be sure to say to you, 'good swimming,'" Mrs. Hemingway wrote in her letter; "and also 'to bring your fishing duds along.'" Mrs. Hemingway wrote other things in the letter. She told him that at last she was prepared to exhibit to him an absolutely true, unsullied, and innocent woman. "A more guileless, immaculate bud of womanhood never blushed on the planet," was one of the several ways in which she phrased the inducement. And to her husband she said triumphantly, "If I don't marry Ned off this time--" leaving unstated the terrible alternative that she lacked either vocabulary to express or imagination to conceive.

Contrary to all her forebodings, Loretta found that she was not unhappy at Santa Clara. Truly, Billy wrote to her every day, but his letters were less distressing than his presence. Also, the ordeal of being away from Daisy was not so severe as she had expected. For the first time in her life she was not lost in eclipse in the blaze of Daisy's brilliant and mature personality. Under such favorable circumstances Loretta came rapidly to the front, while Mrs. Hemingway modestly and shamelessly retreated into the background.

Loretta began to discover that she was not a pale orb shining by reflection. Quite unconsciously she became a small center of things. When she was at the piano, there was someone to turn the pages for her and to express preferences for certain songs. When she dropped her handkerchief, there was someone to pick it up. And there was someone to accompany her in ramblings and flower gatherings. Also, she learned to cast flies in still pools and below savage riffles, and how not to entangle silk lines and gut-leaders with the shrubbery.

Jack Hemingway did not care to teach beginners, and fished much by himself, or not at all, thus giving Ned Bashford ample time in which to consider Loretta as an appearance. As such, she was all that his philosophy demanded. Her blue eyes had the direct gaze of a boy, and out of his profundity he delighted in them and forbore to shudder at the duplicity his philosophy bade him to believe lurked in their depths. She had the grace of a slender flower, the fragility of color and line of fine china, in all of which he pleasured greatly, without thought of the Life Force palpitating beneath and in spite of Bernard Shaw--in whom he believed.

Loretta burgeoned. She swiftly developed personality. She discovered a will of her own and wishes of her own that were not everlastingly entwined with the will and the wishes of Daisy. She was petted by Jack Hemingway, spoiled by Alice Hemingway, and devotedly attended by Ned Bashford. They encouraged her whims and laughed at her follies, while she developed the pretty little tyrannies that are latent in all pretty and delicate women. Her environment acted as a soporific upon her ancient desire always to live with Daisy. This desire no longer prodded her as in the days of her companionship with Billy. The more she saw of Billy, the more certain she had been that she could not live away from Daisy. The more she saw of Ned Bashford, the more she forgot her pressing need of Daisy.

Ned Bashford likewise did some forgetting. He confused superficiality with profundity, and entangled appearance with reality until he accounted them one. Loretta was different from other women. There was no masquerade about her. She was real. He said as much to Mrs. Hemingway, and more, who agreed with him and at the same time caught her husband's eyelid drooping down for the moment in an unmistakable wink.

It was at this time that Loretta received a letter from Billy that was somewhat different from his others. In the main, like all his letters, it was pathological. It was a long recital of symptoms and sufferings, his nervousness, his sleeplessness, and the state of his heart. Then followed reproaches, such as he had never made before. They were sharp enough to make her weep, and true enough to put tragedy into her face. This tragedy she carried down to the breakfast table. It made Jack and Mrs. Hemingway speculative, and it worried Ned. They glanced to him for explanation, but he shook his head.

"I'll find out to-night," Mrs. Hemingway said to her husband.

But Ned caught Loretta in the afternoon in the big living-room. She tried to turn away. He caught her hands, and she faced him with wet lashes and trembling lips. He looked at her, silently and kindly. The lashes grew wetter.

"There, there, don't cry, little one," he said soothingly.

He put his arm protectingly around her shoulder. And to his shoulder, like a tired child, she turned her face. He thrilled in ways unusual for a Greek who has recovered from the long sickness.

"Oh, Ned," she sobbed on his shoulder, "if you only knew how wicked I am!" He smiled indulgently, and breathed in a great breath freighted with the fragrance of her hair. He thought of his world-experience of women, and drew another long breath. There seemed to emanate from her the perfect sweetness of a child--"the aura of a white soul," was the way he phrased it to himself. Then he noticed that her sobs were increasing.

"What's the matter, little one?" he asked pettingly and almost paternally.

"Has Jack been bullying you? Or has your dearly beloved sister failed to write?"

She did not answer, and he felt that he really must kiss her hair, that he could not be responsible if the situation continued much longer.

"Tell me," he said gently, "and we'll see what I can do."

"I can't. You will despise me.--Oh, Ned, I am so ashamed!"

He laughed incredulously, and lightly touched her hair with his lips—so lightly that she did not know.

"Dear little one, let us forget all about it, whatever it is. I want to tell you how I love--" She uttered a sharp cry that was all delight, and then moaned--"Too late!"

"Too late?" he echoed in surprise.

"Oh, why did I? Why did I?" she was moaning. He was aware of a swift chill at his heart.

"What?" he asked.

"Oh, I . . . he . . . Billy.

"I am such a wicked woman, Ned. I know you will never speak to me again."

"This--er--this Billy," he began haltingly. "He is your brother?"

"No . . . he . . . I didn't know. I was so young. I could not help it. Oh, I shall go mad! I shall go mad!"

It was then that Loretta felt his shoulder and the encircling arm become limp. He drew away from her gently, and gently he deposited her in a big chair, where she buried her face and sobbed afresh. He twisted his moustache fiercely, then drew up another chair and sat down.

"I--I do not understand," he said.

"I am so unhappy," she wailed.

"Why unhappy?"

"Because . . . he . . . he wants me to marry him."

His face cleared on the instant, and he placed a hand soothingly on hers.

"That should not make any girl unhappy," he remarked sagely. "Because you don't love him is no reason--of course, you don't love him?"

Loretta shook her head and shoulders in a vigorous negative.

"What?"

Bashford wanted to make sure.

"No," she asserted explosively. "I don't love Billy! I don't want to love Billy!"

"Because you don't love him," Bashford resumed with confidence, "is no reason that you should be unhappy just because he has proposed to you."

She sobbed again, and from the midst of her sobs she cried--

"That's the trouble. I wish I did love him. Oh, I wish I were dead!"

"Now, my dear child, you are worrying yourself over trifles." His other hand crossed over after its mate and rested on hers. "Women do it every day. Because you have changed your mind or did not know your mind, because you have--to use an unnecessarily harsh word--jilted a man--"

"Jilted!" She had raised her head and was looking at him with tear-dimmed eyes. "Oh, Ned, if that were all!"

"All?" he asked in a hollow voice, while his hands slowly retreated from hers. He was about to speak further, then remained silent.

"But I don't want to marry him," Loretta broke forth protestingly.

"Then I shouldn't," he counselled.

"But I ought to marry him."

"OUGHT to marry him?"

She nodded.

"That is a strong word."

"I know it is," she acquiesced, while she strove to control her trembling lips. Then she spoke more calmly. "I am a wicked woman, a terribly wicked woman. No one knows how wicked I am--except Billy."

There was a pause. Ned Bashford's face was grave, and he looked queerly at Loretta.

"He--Billy knows?" he asked finally.

A reluctant nod and flaming cheeks was the reply.

He debated with himself for a while, seeming, like a diver, to be preparing himself for the plunge.

"Tell me about it." He spoke very firmly. "You must tell me all of it."

"And will you--ever--forgive me?" she asked in a faint, small voice.

He hesitated, drew a long breath, and made the plunge.

"Yes," he said desperately. "I'll forgive you. Go ahead."

"There was no one to tell me," she began. "We were with each other so much. I did not know anything of the world--then."

She paused to meditate. Bashford was biting his lip impatiently.

"If I had only known--"

She paused again.

"Yes, go on," he urged.

"We were together almost every evening."

"Billy?" he demanded, with a savageness that startled her.

"Yes, of course, Billy. We were with each other so much . . . If I had only known . . . There was no one to tell me . . . I was so young--"

Her lips parted as though to speak further, and she regarded him anxiously.

"The scoundrel!"

With the explosion Ned Bashford was on his feet, no longer a tired Greek, but a violently angry young man.

"Billy is not a scoundrel; he is a good man," Loretta defended, with a firmness that surprised Bashford.

"I suppose you'll be telling me next that it was all your fault," he said sarcastically.

She nodded.

"What?" he shouted.

"It was all my fault," she said steadily. "I should never have let him. I was to blame."

Bashford ceased from his pacing up and down, and when he spoke, his voice was resigned.

"All right," he said. "I don't blame you in the least, Loretta. And you have been very honest. But Billy is right, and you are wrong. You must get married."

"To Billy?" she asked, in a dim, far-away voice.

"Yes, to Billy. I'll see to it. Where does he live? I'll make him."

"But I don't want to marry Billy!" she cried out in alarm. "Oh, Ned, you won't do that?"

"I shall," he answered sternly. "You must. And Billy must. Do you understand?"

Loretta buried her face in the cushioned chair back, and broke into a passionate storm of sobs.

All that Bashford could make out at first, as he listened, was: "But I don't want to leave Daisy! I don't want to leave Daisy!"

He paced grimly back and forth, then stopped curiously to listen.

"How was I to know?--Boo--hoo," Loretta was crying. "He didn't tell me. Nobody else ever kissed me. I never dreamed a kiss could be so terrible . . . until, boo-hoo . . . until he wrote to me. I only got the letter this morning."

His face brightened. It seemed as though light was dawning on him.

"Is that what you're crying about?"

"N--no."

His heart sank.

"Then what are you crying about?" he asked in a hopeless voice.

"Because you said I had to marry Billy. And I don't want to marry Billy. I don't want to leave Daisy. I don't know what I want. I wish I were dead."

He nerved himself for another effort.

"Now look here, Loretta, be sensible. What is this about kisses? You haven't told me everything?"

"I--I don't want to tell you everything."

She looked at him beseechingly in the silence that fell.

"Must I?" she quavered finally.

"You must," he said imperatively. "You must tell me everything."

"Well, then . . . must I?"

"You must."

"He . . . I . . . we . . ." she began flounderingly. Then blurted out, "I let him, and he kissed me."

"Go on," Bashford commanded desperately.

"That's all," she answered.

"All?" There was a vast incredulity in his voice.

"All?" In her voice was an interrogation no less vast.

"I mean--er--nothing worse?" He was overwhelmingly aware of his own awkwardness.

"Worse?" She was frankly puzzled. "As though there could be! Billy said--"

"When did he say it?" Bashford demanded abruptly.

"In his letter I got this morning. Billy said that my . . . our . . . our kisses were terrible if we didn't get married."

Bashford's head was swimming.

"What else did Billy say?" he asked.

"He said that when a woman allowed a man to kiss her, she always married him--that it was terrible if she didn't. It was the custom, he said; and I say it is a bad, wicked custom, and I don't like it. I know I'm terrible," she added defiantly, "but I can't help it."

Bashford absent-mindedly brought out a cigarette.

"Do you mind if I smoke?" he asked, as he struck a match.

Then he came to himself.

"I beg your pardon," he cried, flinging away match and cigarette. "I don't want to smoke. I didn't mean that at all. What I mean is--"

He bent over Loretta, caught her hands in his, then sat on the arm of the chair and softly put one arm around her.

"Loretta, I am a fool. I mean it. And I mean something more. I want you to be my wife."

He waited anxiously in the pause that followed.

"You might answer me," he urged.

"I will . . . if--"

"Yes, go on. If what?"

"If I don't have to marry Billy."

"You can't marry both of us," he almost shouted.

"And it isn't the custom . . . what. . . what Billy said?"

"No, it isn't the custom. Now, Loretta, will you marry me?"

"Don't be angry with me," she pouted demurely.

He gathered her into his arms and kissed her.

"I wish it were the custom," she said in a faint voice, from the midst of the embrace, "because then I'd have to marry you, Ned dear . . . wouldn't I?"

THE MASQUE OF RED DEATH

The red death had long devastated the country. No pestilence had ever been so fatal, or so hideous. Blood was its Avatar and its seal--the madness and the horror of blood. There were sharp pains, and sudden dizziness, and then profuse bleeding at the pores, with dissolution. The scarlet stains upon the body and especially upon the face of the victim, were the pest ban which shut him out from the aid and from the sympathy of his fellow-men. And the whole seizure, progress, and termination of the disease, were incidents of half an hour.

But Prince Prospero was happy and dauntless and sagacious. When his dominions were half depopulated, he summoned to his presence a thousand hale and light-hearted friends from among the knights and dames of his court, and with these retired to the deep seclusion of one of his crenellated abbeys. This was an extensive and magnificent structure, the creation of the prince's own eccentric yet august taste. A strong and lofty wall girdled it in. This wall had gates of iron. The courtiers, having entered, brought furnaces and massy hammers and welded the bolts.

They resolved to leave means neither of ingress nor egress to the sudden impulses of despair or of frenzy from within. The abbey was amply provisioned. With such precautions the courtiers might bid defiance to contagion. The external world could take care of itself. In the meantime, it was folly to grieve or to think. The prince had provided all the appliances of pleasure. There were buffoons, there were improvisatori, there were ballet-dancers, there were musicians, there was Beauty, there was wine. All these and security were within. Without was the "Red Death." It was toward the close of the fifth or sixth month of his seclusion that the Prince Prospero entertained his thousand friends at a masked ball of the most unusual magnificence.

It was a voluptuous scene, that masquerade. But first let me tell of the rooms in which it was held. There were seven--an imperial suite, in many palaces, however, such suites form a long and straight vista, while the folding doors slide back nearly to the walls on either hand, so that the view of the whole extant is scarcely impeded. Here the case was very different; as might have been expected from the duke's love of the "bizarre." The apartments were so irregularly disposed that the vision embraced but little more than one at a time. There was a sharp turn at the right and left, in the middle of each wall, a tall and narrow Gothic window looked out upon a closed corridor of which pursued the windings of the suite. These windows were of stained glass whose color varied in accordance with the prevailing hue of the decorations of the chamber into which it opened. That at the eastern extremity was hung, for example, in blue--and vividly blue were its windows. The second chamber was purple in its ornaments and tapestries, and here the panes were purple. The third was green throughout, and so were the casements. The fourth was furnished and lighted with orange--the fifth with white--the sixth with violet. The seventh apartment was closely shrouded in black velvet tapestries that hung all over the ceiling and down the walls, falling in heavy folds upon a carpet of the same material and hue. But in this chamber only, the color of the windows failed to correspond with the decorations.

The panes were scarlet--a deep blood color. Now in no one of any of the seven apartments was there any lamp or candelabrum, amid the profusion of golden ornaments that lay scattered to and fro and depended from the roof. There was no light of any kind emanating from lamp or candle within the suite of chambers. But in the corridors that followed the suite, there stood, opposite each window, a heavy tripod, bearing a brazier of fire, that projected its rays through the tinted glass and so glaringly lit the room. And thus were produced a multitude of gaudy and fantastic appearances.

But in the western or back chamber the effect of the fire-light that streamed upon the dark hangings through the blood-tinted panes was ghastly in the extreme, and produced so wild a look upon the countenances of those who entered, that there were few of the company bold enough to set foot within its precincts at all. It was within this apartment, also, that there stood against the western wall, a gigantic clock of ebony. It pendulum swung to and fro with a dull, heavy, monotonous clang; and when the minute-hand made the circuit of the face, and the hour was to be stricken, there came from the brazen lungs of the clock a sound which was clear and loud and deep and exceedingly musical, but of so peculiar a note and emphasis that, at each lapse of an hour, the musicians of the orchestra were constrained to pause, momentarily, in their performance, to hearken to the sound; and thus the waltzers perforce ceased their evolutions; and there was a brief disconcert of the whole gay company; and while the chimes of the clock yet rang.

It was observed that the giddiest grew pale, and the more aged and sedate passed their hands over their brows as if in confused reverie or meditation. But when the echoes had fully ceased, a light laughter at once pervaded the assembly; the musicians looked at each other and smiled as if at their own nervousness and folly, and made whispering vows, each to the other, that the next chiming of the clock should produce in them no similar emotion; and then, after the lapse of sixty minutes (which embrace three thousand and six hundred seconds of Time that flies), there came yet another chiming of the clock, and then were the same disconcert and tremulousness and meditation as before. But, in spite of these things, it was a gay and magnificent revel. The tastes of the duke were peculiar.

He had a fine eye for color and effects. He disregarded the "decora" of mere fashion. His plans were bold and fiery, and his conceptions glowed with barbaric luster. There are some who would have thought him mad. His followers felt that he was not. It was necessary to hear and see and touch him to be _sure_ he was not.

He had directed, in great part, the movable embellishments of the seven chambers, upon occasion of this great fete; and it was his own guiding taste which had given character to the masqueraders. Be sure they were grotesque. There were much glare and glitter and piquancy and phantasm--much of what has been seen in "Hernani." There were arabesque figures with unsuited limbs and appointments. There were delirious fancies such as the madman fashions. There were much of the beautiful, much of the wanton, much of the bizarre, something of the terrible, and not a little of that which might have excited disgust.

To and fro in the seven chambers stalked, in fact, a multitude of dreams. And these the dreams--writhed in and about, taking hue from the rooms, and causing the wild music of the orchestra to seem as the echo of their steps. And, anon, there strikes the ebony clock which stands in the hall of the velvet. And then, for a moment, all is still, and all is silent save the voice of the clock. The dreams are stiff-frozen as they stand. But the echoes of the chime die away--they have endured but an instant--and a light half-subdued laughter floats after them as they depart.

And now the music swells, and the dreams live, and writhe to and fro more merrily than ever, taking hue from the many-tinted windows through which stream the rays of the tripods. But to the chamber which lies most westwardly of the seven there are now none of the maskers who venture, for the night is waning away; and there flows a ruddier light through the blood-colored panes; and the blackness of the sable drapery appalls; and to him whose foot falls on the sable carpet, there comes from the near clock of ebony a muffled peal more solemnly emphatic than any which reaches _their_ ears who indulge in the more remote gaieties of the other apartments.

But these other apartments were densely crowded, and in them beat feverishly the heart of life. And the revel went whirlingly on, until at length there commenced the sounding of midnight upon the clock. And then the music ceased, as I have told; and the evolutions of the waltzers were quieted; and there was an uneasy cessation of all things as before. But now there were twelve strokes to be sounded by the bell of the clock; and thus it happened, perhaps that more of thought crept, with more of time into the meditations of the thoughtful among those who reveled. And thus too, it happened, that before the last echoes of the last chime had utterly sunk into silence, there were many individuals in the crowd who had found leisure to become aware of the presence of a masked figure which had arrested the attention of no single individual before.

And the rumor of this new presence having spread itself whisperingly around, there arose at length from the whole company a buzz, or murmur, of horror, and of disgust.   In an assembly of phantasms such as I have painted, it may well be supposed that no ordinary appearance could have excited such sensation. In truth the masquerade license of the night was nearly unlimited; but the figure in question had out-Heroded Herod, and gone beyond the bounds of even the prince's indefinite decorum.

There are chords in the hearts of the most reckless which cannot be touched without emotion. Even with the utterly lost, to whom life and death are equally jests, there are matters of which no jest can be made. The whole company, indeed, seemed now deeply to feel that in the costume and bearing of the stranger neither wit nor propriety existed. The figure was tall and gaunt, and shrouded from head to foot in the habiliments of the grave. The mask which concealed the visage was made so nearly to resemble the countenance of a stiffened corpse that the closest scrutiny must have difficulty in detecting the cheat.

And yet all this might have been endured, if not approved, by the mad revelers around. But the mummer had gone so far as to assume the type of the Red Death. His vesture was dabbled in _blood_--and his broad brow, with all the features of his face, was besprinkled with the scarlet horror. When the eyes of Prince Prospero fell on this spectral image (which, with a slow and solemn movement, as if more fully to sustain its role, stalked to and fro among the waltzers) he was seen to be convulsed, in the first moment with a strong shudder either of terror or distaste; but in the next, his brow reddened with rage. "Who dares"--he demanded hoarsely of the courtiers who stood near him--"who dares insult us with this blasphemous mockery? Seize him and unmask him--that we may know whom we have to hang, at sunrise, from the battlements!" It was in the eastern or blue chamber in which stood Prince Prospero as he uttered these words. They rang throughout the seven rooms loudly and clearly, for the prince was a bold and robust man, and the music had become hushed at the waving of his hand.

It was in the blue room where stood the prince, with a group of pale courtiers by his side. At first, as he spoke, there was a slight rushing movement of this group in the direction of the intruder, who, at the moment was also near at hand, and now, with deliberate and stately step, made closer approach to the speaker. But from a certain nameless awe with which the mad assumptions of the mummer had inspired the whole party, there were found none who put forth a hand to seize him; so that, unimpeded, he passed within a yard of the prince's person; and while the vast assembly, as with one impulse, shrank from the centers of the rooms to the walls, he made his way uninterruptedly, but with the same solemn and measured step which had distinguished him from the first, through the blue chamber to the purple--to the purple to the green--through the green to the orange--through this again to the white--and even thence to the violet, ere a decided movement had been made to arrest him.

It was then, however, that the Prince Prospero, maddened with rage and the shame of his own momentary cowardice, rushed hurriedly through the six chambers, while none followed him on account of a deadly terror that had seized upon all. He bore aloft a drawn dagger, and had approached, in rapid impetuosity, to within three or four feet of the retreating figure, when the latter, having attained the extremity of the velvet apartment, turned suddenly and confronted his pursuer. There was a sharp cry--and the dagger dropped gleaming upon the sable carpet, upon which most instantly afterward, fell prostrate in death the Prince Prospero.

Then summoning the wild courage of despair, a throng of the revelers at once threw themselves into the black apartment, and seizing the mummer whose tall figure stood erect and motionless within the shadow of the ebony clock, gasped in unutterable horror at finding the grave cerements and corpse-like mask, which they handled with so violent a rudeness, untenanted by any tangible form. And now was acknowledged the presence of the red death. He had come like a thief in the night. And one by one dropped the revelers in the blood-bedewed halls of their revel, and died each in the despairing posture of his fall. And the life of the ebony clock went out with that of the last of the gay. And the flames of the tripods expired. And darkness and decay and the red death held illimitable dominion over all.

THE VALLEY OF SPIDERS

Towards mid-day the three pursuers came abruptly round a bend in the torrent bed upon the sight of a very broad and spacious valley. The difficult and winding trench of pebbles along which they had tracked the fugitives for so long, expanded to a broad slope, and with a common impulse the three men left the trail, and rode to a little eminence set with olive-dun trees, and there halted, the two others, as became them, a little behind the man with the silver-studded bridle.

For a space they scanned the great expanse below them with eager eyes. It spread remoter and remoter, with only a few clusters of sere thorn bushes here and there, and the dim suggestions of some now waterless ravine, to break its desolation of yellow grass. Its purple distances melted at last into the bluish slopes of the further hills--hills it might be of a greener kind--and above them invisibly supported, and seeming indeed to hang in the blue, were the snowclad summits of mountains that grew larger and bolder to the north-westward as the sides of the valley drew together. And westward the valley opened until a distant darkness under the sky told where the forests began. But the three men looked neither east nor west, but only steadfastly across the valley.

The gaunt man with the scarred lip was the first to speak. "Nowhere," he said, with a sigh of disappointment in his voice.

"But after all, they had a full day's start."

"They don't know we are after them," said the little man on the white horse.

"SHE would know," said the leader bitterly, as if speaking to himself.

"Even then they can't go fast. They've got no beast but the mule, and all to-day the girl's foot has been bleeding---"

The man with the silver bridle flashed a quick intensity of rage on him. "Do you think I haven't seen that?" he snarled.

"It helps, anyhow," whispered the little man to himself.

The gaunt man with the scarred lip stared impassively. "They can't be over the valley," he said. "If we ride hard--" He glanced at the white horse and paused.

"Curse all white horses!" said the man with the silver bridle,
and turned to scan the beast his curse included.

The little man looked down between the melancholy ears of his steed.

"I did my best," he said.

The two others stared again across the valley for a space. The gaunt man
passed the back of his hand across the scarred lip.

"Come up!" said the man who owned the silver bridle, suddenly.

The little man started and jerked his rein, and the horse hoofs of the three
made a multitudinous faint pattering upon the withered grass as they turned
back towards the trail. . . .

They rode cautiously down the long slope before them, and so came
through a waste of prickly, twisted bushes and strange dry shapes of horny
branches that grew amongst the rocks, into the levels below. And there the
trail grew faint, for the soil was scanty, and the only herbage was this scorched
dead straw that lay upon the ground. Still, by hard scanning, by leaning beside
the horses' necks and pausing ever and again, even these white men could
contrive to follow after their prey.

There were trodden places, bent and broken blades of the coarse grass,
and ever and again the sufficient intimation of a footmark. And once the
leader saw a brown smear of blood where the half-caste girl may have trod.
And at that under his breath he cursed her for a fool.

The gaunt man checked his leader's tracking, and the little man on the
white horse rode behind, a man lost in a dream. They rode one after another,
the man with the silver bridle led the way, and they spoke never a word. After
a time, it came to the little man on the white horse that the world was very
still. He started out of his dream. Besides the little noises of their horses and
equipment, the whole great valley kept the brooding quiet of a painted scene.

Before him went his master and his fellow, each intently leaning forward to the left, each impassively moving with the paces of his horse; their shadows went before them--still, noiseless, tapering attendants; and nearer a crouched cool shape was his own. He looked about him. What was it had gone? Then he remembered the reverberation from the banks of the gorge and the perpetual accompaniment of shifting, jostling pebbles. And, moreover--? There was no breeze. That was it! What a vast, still place it was, a monotonous afternoon slumber. And the sky open and blank, except for a somber veil of haze that had gathered in the upper valley.

He straightened his back, fretted with his bridle, puckered his lips to whistle, and simply sighed. He turned in his saddle for a time, and stared at the throat of the mountain gorge out of which they had come. Blank! Blank slopes on either side, with never a sign of a decent beast or tree--much less a man. What a land it was! What a wilderness! He dropped again into his former pose.

It filled him with a momentary pleasure to see a wry stick of purple black flash out into the form of a snake, and vanish amidst the brown. After all, the infernal valley WAS alive. And then, to rejoice him still more, came a little breath across his face, a whisper that came and went, the faintest inclination of a stiff black-antlered bush upon a little crest, the first intimations of a possible breeze.

Idly he wetted his finger, and held it up. He pulled up sharply to avoid a collision with the gaunt man, who had stopped at fault upon the trail. Just at that guilty moment he caught his master's eye looking towards him.

For a time, he forced an interest in the tracking. Then, as they rode on again, he studied his master's shadow and hat and shoulder, appearing and disappearing behind the gaunt man's nearer contours. They had ridden four days out of the very limits of the world into this desolate place, short of water, with nothing but a strip of dried meat under their saddles, over rocks and mountains, where surely none but these fugitives had ever been before--for THAT!

And all this was for a girl, a mere willful child! And the man had whole cityfulls of people to do his basest bidding--girls, women! Why in the name of passionate folly THIS one in particular? Asked the little man, and scowled at the world, and licked his parched lips with a blackened tongue. It was the way of the master, and that was all he knew. Just because she sought to evade him. . . .

His eye caught a whole row of high plumed canes bending in unison, and then the tails of silk that hung before his neck flapped and fell. The breeze was growing stronger. Somehow it took the stiff stillness out of things--and that was well.

"Hullo!" said the gaunt man.

All three stopped abruptly.

"What?" asked the master. "What?"

"Over there," said the gaunt man, pointing up the valley.

"What?"

"Something coming towards us."

And as he spoke a yellow animal crested a rise and came bearing down upon them. It was a big wild dog, coming before the wind, tongue out, at a steady pace, and running with such an intensity of purpose that he did not seem to see the horsemen he approached. He ran with his nose up, following, it was plain, neither scent nor quarry. As he drew nearer the little man felt for his sword.

"He's mad," said the gaunt rider.

"Shout!" said the little man, and shouted.

The dog came on. Then when the little man's blade was already out, it swerved aside and went panting by them and past. The eyes of the little man followed its flight. "There was no foam," he said. For a space the man with the silver-studded bridle stared up the valley. "Oh, come on!" he cried at last. "What does it matter?" and jerked his horse into movement again.

The little man left the insoluble mystery of a dog that fled from nothing but the wind, and lapsed into profound musings on human character. "Come on!" he whispered to himself. "Why should it be given to one man to say 'Come on!' with that stupendous violence of effect. Always, all his life, the man with the silver bridle has been saying that. If _I_ said it--!" thought the little man.

But people marveled when the master was disobeyed even in the wildest things. This half-caste girl seemed to him, seemed to everyone, mad--blasphemous almost. The little man, by way of comparison, reflected on the gaunt rider with the scarred lip, as stalwart as his master, as brave and, indeed, perhaps braver, and yet for him there was obedience, nothing but to give obedience duly and stoutly. . .

Certain sensations of the hands and knees called the little man back to more immediate things. He became aware of something. He rode up beside his gaunt fellow. "Do you notice the horses?" he said in an undertone.

The gaunt face looked interrogation.

"They don't like this wind," said the little man, and dropped behind as the man with the silver bridle turned upon him.

"It's all right," said the gaunt-faced man.

They rode on again for a space in silence. The foremost two rode downcast upon the trail, the hindmost man watched the haze that crept down the vastness of the valley, nearer and nearer, and noted how the wind grew in strength moment by moment. Far away on the left he saw a line of dark bulks--wild hog perhaps, galloping down the valley, but of that he said nothing, nor did he remark again upon the uneasiness of the horses.

And then he saw first one and then a second great white ball, a great shining white ball like a gigantic head of thistle-down, that drove before the wind athwart the path. These balls soared high in the air, and dropped and rose again and caught for a moment, and hurried on and passed, but at the sight of them the restlessness of the horses increased.

Then presently he saw that more of these drifting globes--and then soon very many more--were hurrying towards him down the valley. They became aware of a squealing. Athwart the path a huge boar rushed, turning his head but for one instant to glance at them, and then hurling on down the valley again. And at that, all three stopped and sat in their saddles, staring into the thickening haze that was coming upon them.

"If it were not for this thistle-down--" began the leader.

But now a big globe came drifting past within a score of yards of them. It was really not an even sphere at all, but a vast, soft, ragged, filmy thing, a sheet gathered by the corners, an aerial jelly-fish, as it were, but rolling over and over as it advanced, and trailing long, cobwebby threads and streamers that floated in its wake.

"It isn't thistle-down," said the little man.

"I don't like the stuff," said the gaunt man.

And they looked at one another.

"Curse it!" cried the leader. "The air's full of it up there.
If it keeps on at this pace long, it will stop us altogether."

An instinctive feeling, such as lines out a herd of deer at the approach of some ambiguous thing, prompted them to turn their horses to the wind, ride forward for a few paces, and stare at that advancing multitude of floating masses. They came on before the wind with a sort of smooth swiftness, rising and falling noiselessly, sinking to earth, rebounding high, soaring--all with a perfect unanimity, with a still, deliberate assurance.

Right and left of the horsemen the pioneers of this strange army passed. At one that rolled along the ground, breaking shapelessly and trailing out reluctantly into long grappling ribbons and bands, all three horses began to shy and dance. The master was seized with a sudden unreasonable impatience. He cursed the drifting globes roundly. "Get on!" he cried; "get on! What do these things matter? How CAN they matter? Back to the trail!" He fell swearing at his horse and sawed the bit across its mouth.

He shouted aloud with rage. "I will follow that trail, I tell you!" he cried. "Where is the trail?"

He gripped the bridle of his prancing horse and searched amidst the grass. A long and clinging thread fell across his face, a grey streamer dropped about his bridle-arm, some big, active thing with many legs ran down the back of his head. He looked up to discover one of those grey masses anchored as it were above him by these things and flapping out ends as a sail flaps when a boat comes, about--but noiselessly.

He had an impression of many eyes, of a dense crew of squat bodies, of long, many-jointed limbs hauling at their mooring ropes to bring the thing down upon him. For a space he stared up, reining in his prancing horse with the instinct born of years of horsemanship. Then the flat of a sword smote his back, and a blade flashed overhead and cut the drifting balloon of spider-web free, and the whole mass lifted softly and drove clear and away.

"Spiders!" cried the voice of the gaunt man. "The things are full of big spiders! Look, my lord!"

The man with the silver bridle still followed the mass that drove away.

"Look, my lord!"

The master found himself staring down at a red, smashed thing on the ground that, in spite of partial obliteration, could still wriggle unavailing legs. Then when the gaunt man pointed to another mass that bore down upon them, he drew his sword hastily. Up the valley now it was like a fog bank torn to rags. He tried to grasp the situation.

"Ride for it!" the little man was shouting. "Ride for it down the valley."

What happened then was like the confusion of a battle. The man with the silver bridle saw the little man go past him slashing furiously at imaginary cobwebs, saw him cannon into the horse of the gaunt man and hurl it and its rider to earth. His own horse went a dozen paces before he could rein it in. Then he looked up to avoid imaginary dangers, and then back again to see a horse rolling on the ground, the gaunt man standing and slashing over it at a rent and fluttering mass of grey that streamed and wrapped about them both. And thick and fast as thistle-down on waste land on a windy day in July, the cobweb masses were coming on.

The little man had dismounted, but he dared not release his horse. He was endeavoring to lug the struggling brute back with the strength of one arm, while with the other he slashed aimlessly, the tentacles of a second grey mass had entangled themselves with the struggle, and this second grey mass came to its moorings, and slowly sank.

The master set his teeth, gripped his bridle, lowered his head, and spurred his horse forward. The horse on the ground rolled over, there were blood and moving shapes upon the flanks, and the gaunt man, suddenly leaving it, ran forward towards his master, perhaps ten paces. His legs were swathed and encumbered with grey; he made ineffectual movements with his sword. Grey streamers waved from him; there was a thin veil of grey across his face. With his left hand he beat at something on his body, and suddenly he stumbled and fell. He struggled to rise, and fell again, and suddenly, horribly, began to howl, "Oh--ohoo, ohooh!"

The master could see the great spiders upon him, and others upon the ground.

As he strove to force his horse nearer to this gesticulating, screaming grey object that struggled up and down, there came a clatter of hoofs, and the little man, in act of mounting, sword less, balanced on his belly athwart the white horse, and clutching its mane, whirled past. And again a clinging thread of grey gossamer swept across the master's face. All about him, and over him, it seemed this drifting, noiseless cobweb circled and drew nearer him. . . .

To the day of his death he never knew just how the event of that moment happened. Did he, indeed, turn his horse, or did it really of its own accord stampede after its fellow? Suffice it that in another second he was galloping full tilt down the valley with his sword whirling furiously overhead. And all about him on the quickening breeze, the spiders' airships, their air bundles and air sheets, seemed to him to hurry in a conscious pursuit.

Clatter, clatter, thud, thud--the man with the silver bridle rode, heedless of his direction, with his fearful face looking up now right, now left, and his sword arm ready to slash. And a few hundred yards ahead of him, with a tail of torn cobweb trailing behind him, rode the little man on the white horse, still but imperfectly in the saddle. The reeds bent before them, the wind blew fresh and strong, over his shoulder the master could see the webs hurrying to overtake. . . .

He was so intent to escape the spiders' webs that only as his horse gathered together for a leap did he realize the ravine ahead. And then he raised it only to misunderstand and interfere. He was leaning forward on his horse's neck and sat up and back all too late.

But if in his excitement he had failed to leap, at any rate he had not forgotten how to fall. He was horseman again in mid-air. He came off clear with a mere bruise upon his shoulder, and his horse rolled, kicking spasmodic legs, and lay still. But the master's sword drove its point into the hard soil, and snapped clean across, as though Chance refused him any longer as her Knight, and the splintered end missed his face by an inch or so.

He was on his feet in a moment, breathlessly scanning the onrushing spider-webs. For a moment he was minded to run, and then thought of the ravine, and turned back. He ran aside once to dodge one drifting terror, and then he was swiftly clambering down the precipitous sides, and out of the touch of the gale.

There under the lee of the dry torrent's steeper banks he might crouch, and watch these strange, grey masses pass and pass in safety till the wind fell, and it became possible to escape. And there for a long time he crouched, watching the strange, grey, ragged masses trail their streamers across his narrowed sky.

Once a stray spider fell into the ravine close beside him--a full foot it measured from leg to leg, and its body was half a man's hand--and after he had watched its monstrous alacrity of search and escape for a little while, and tempted it to bite his broken sword, he lifted up his iron-heeled boot and smashed it into a pulp. He swore as he did so, and for a time sought up and down for another.

Then presently, when he was surer these spider swarms could not drop into the ravine, he found a place where he could sit down, and sat and fell into deep thought and began after his manner to gnaw his knuckles and bite his nails. And from this he was moved by the coming of the man with the white horse.

He heard him long before he saw him, as a clattering of hoofs, stumbling footsteps, and a reassuring voice. Then the little man appeared, a rueful figure, still with a tail of white cobweb trailing behind him. They approached each other without speaking, without a salutation. The little man was fatigued and shamed to the pitch of hopeless bitterness, and came to a stop at last, face to face with his seated master. The latter winced a little under his dependent's eye. "Well?" he said at last, with no pretense of authority.

"You left him?"

"My horse bolted."

"I know. So did mine."

He laughed at his master mirthlessly.

"I say my horse bolted," said the man who once had a silver-studded bridle.

"Cowards both," said the little man.

The other gnawed his knuckle through some meditative moments, with his eye on his inferior.

"Don't call me a coward," he said at length.

"You are a coward like myself."

"A coward possibly. There is a limit beyond which every man must fear.

69

That I have learnt at last. But not like yourself. That is where the difference comes in."

"I never could have dreamt you would have left him. He saved your life two minutes before. . . . Why are you our lord?"

The master gnawed his knuckles again, and his countenance was dark.

"No man calls me a coward," he said. "No. A broken sword is better than none. . . . One spavined white horse cannot be expected to carry two men a four days' journey. I hate white horses, but this time it cannot be helped. You begin to understand me? . . . I perceive that you are minded, on the strength of what you have seen and fancy, to taint my reputation. It is men of your sort who unmake kings. Besides which--I never liked you."

"My lord!" said the little man.

"No," said the master. "NO!"

He stood up sharply as the little man moved. For a minute perhaps they faced one another. Overhead the spiders' balls went driving. There was a quick movement among the pebbles; a running of feet, a cry of despair, a gasp and a blow. . . .

Towards nightfall the wind fell. The sun set in a calm serenity, and the man who had once possessed the silver bridle came at last very cautiously and by an easy slope out of the ravine again; but now he led the white horse that once belonged to the little man.

He would have gone back to his horse to get his silver-mounted bridle again, but he feared night and a quickening breeze might still find him in the valley, and besides he disliked greatly to think he might discover his horse all swathed in cobwebs and perhaps unpleasantly eaten.

And as he thought of those cobwebs and of all the dangers he had been through, and the manner in which he had been preserved that day, his hand sought a little reliquary that hung about his neck, and he clasped it for a moment with heartfelt gratitude. As he did so his eyes went across the valley.

"I was hot with passion," he said, "and now she has met her reward. They also, no doubt--"

And behold! Far away out of the wooded slopes across the valley, but in the clearness of the sunset distinct and unmistakable, he saw a little spire of smoke.

At that his expression of serene resignation changed to an amazed anger. Smoke? He turned the head of the white horse about, and hesitated. And as he did so a little rustle of air went through the grass about him. Far away upon some reeds swayed a tattered sheet of grey. He looked at the cobwebs; he looked at the smoke.

"Perhaps, after all, it is not them," he said at last.

But he knew better.

After he had stared at the smoke for some time, he mounted the white horse.

As he rode, he picked his way amidst stranded masses of web. For some reason there were many dead spiders on the ground, and those that lived feasted guiltily on their fellows. At the sound of his horse's hoofs they fled.

Their time had passed. From the ground without either a wind to carry them or a winding sheet ready, these things, for all their poison, could do him little evil. He flicked with his belt at those he fancied came too near. Once, where a number ran together over a bare place, he was minded to dismount and trample them with his boots, but this impulse he overcame. Ever and again he turned in his saddle, and looked back at the smoke.

"Spiders," he muttered over and over again. "Spiders! Well, well. . . . The next time I must spin a web."

A HAUNTED HOUSE

Whatever hour you woke there was a door shutting. From room to room they went, hand in hand, lifting here, opening there, making sure--a ghostly couple.

"Here we left it," she said. And he added, "Oh, but here too!" "It's upstairs," she murmured. "And in the garden," he whispered. "Quietly," they said, "or we shall wake them."

But it wasn't that you woke us. Oh, no. "They're looking for it; they're drawing the curtain," one might say, and so read on a page or two. "Now they've found it,' one would be certain, stopping the pencil on the margin. And then, tired of reading, one might rise and see for oneself, the house all empty, the doors standing open, only the wood pigeons bubbling with content and the hum of the threshing machine sounding from the farm. "What did I come in here for? What did I want to find?" My hands were empty. "Perhaps its upstairs then?" The apples were in the loft. And so down again, the garden still as ever, only the book had slipped into the grass.

But they had found it in the drawing room. Not that one could ever see them. The windowpanes reflected apples, reflected roses; all the leaves were green in the glass. If they moved in the drawing room, the apple only turned its yellow side. Yet, the moment after, if the door was opened, spread about the floor, hung upon the walls, pendant from the ceiling--what? My hands were empty. The shadow of a thrush crossed the carpet; from the deepest wells of silence the wood pigeon drew its bubble of sound. "Safe, safe, safe" the pulse of the house beat softly. "The treasure buried; the room . . ." the pulse stopped short. Oh, was that the buried treasure?

A moment later the light had faded. Out in the garden then? But the trees spun darkness for a wandering beam of sun. So fine, so rare, coolly sunk beneath the surface the beam I sought always burned behind the glass. Death was the glass; death was between us, coming to the woman first, hundreds of years ago, leaving the house, sealing all the windows; the rooms were darkened. He left it, left her, went North, went East, saw the stars turned in the Southern sky; sought the house, found it dropped beneath the Downs. "Safe, safe, safe," the pulse of the house beat gladly. 'The Treasure yours."

The wind roars up the avenue. Trees stoop and bend this way and that. Moonbeams splash and spill wildly in the rain. But the beam of the lamp falls straight from the window. The candle burns stiff and still. Wandering through the house, opening the windows, whispering not to wake us, the ghostly couple seek their joy.

"Here we slept," she says. And he adds, "Kisses without number." "Waking in the morning--" "Silver between the trees--" "Upstairs--" 'In the garden--" "When summer came--" 'In winter snow time--" "The doors go shutting far in the distance, gently knocking like the pulse of a heart.

Nearer they come, cease at the doorway. The wind falls, the rain slides silver down the glass. Our eyes darken, we hear no steps beside us; we see no lady spread her ghostly cloak. His hands shield the lantern. "Look," he breathes. "Sound asleep. Love upon their lips."

Stooping, holding their silver lamp above us, long they look and deeply. Long they pause. The wind drives straightly; the flame stoops slightly. Wild beams of moonlight cross both floor and wall, and, meeting, stain the faces bent; the faces pondering; the faces that search the sleepers and seek their hidden joy.

"Safe, safe, safe," the heart of the house beats proudly. "Long years--" he sighs. "Again you found me." "Here," she murmurs, "sleeping; in the garden reading; laughing, rolling apples in the loft. Here we left our treasure--" Stooping, their light lifts the lids upon my eyes. "Safe! safe! safe!" the pulse of the house beats wildly. Waking, I cry "Oh, is this your buried treasure? The light in the heart."

~ TRUE STORIES ~

EXPERIENCES FROM REAL PEOPLE

The following stories are from real people who are remembering an account of their experiences. We'll never know if they're completely true or imagined, but they will give you the creeps none the less.

THE THREE AM EXPERIENCE

When I was seven, I was sleeping in my parent's room because I didn't have my own room at the time. My dad was working at the casino down in Laughlin, which was about 30 minutes away from my house at the time in a housing complex where every house looked exactly the same, except with different colored shackles on the top of the houses.

It was around 2:32 in the morning when I woke up to go to the bathroom, and get a glass of water before going back to sleep. I spent a while in the bathroom, and since I didn't have a phone at the time, I was playing with my old "Spongebob knows your name" doll from around 2001.

I was a complete spongebob fan, as I had Patrick and Squidward toys in my house's computer room. where all the toys of mine were kept in the closet. I finished going to the bathroom and proceeded to go out to the kitchen where my Grandfather was asleep and left the Television on. I just left it on, as he tends to keep it on 24/7.

It seemed a bit tense in the kitchen, but I just ignored it. I poured myself a glass of water from our old water dispenser from when we lived in Tucson. I went back to my parent's room and I laid back down after drinking my water. Around 10 minutes passed, and I couldn't fall back to sleep. I looked for my mother's iPad, which I usually just watch YouTube videos until I fall asleep.

I found the iPad case, opened it, and it was dead. I put it back where I found it, and just laid there. Two minutes passed, and I suddenly had the urge to sit up. I followed the urge and sat up, stuck staring in the corner where my parent's lamp is. It turned off randomly, and I saw some black figure.

It choked me until I could wake up my mother, who was right next to me on the bed. She got up, and I could barely speak. I was completely out of breath. She grabbed me and ran into the living room where my grandfather was sleeping, and told me to sleep out there for the rest of the night. The exact day after that, I was sitting on the couch with my SpongeBob doll and my woody doll.

My woody doll wouldn't stop going off, so we had to take out the batteries. A few hours after that, the woody doll went off again, but this time in a much louder manner, to where you could hear it from all the way from the back of my house. It just said "Reach for the sky.". I grabbed it and checked the batteries after it was done saying the phrase.

The batteries weren't even in there, so it just makes it even more confusing, not to mention that my SpongeBob doll said "I'm going to kill you, James!", which is my name, but was never programmed into the doll, nor was the phrase. So it just makes it even more creepier. I'm 12 now, and every time I wake up at around 3 A.M., I feel something watching over me.

LADY OF THE HOLLOW

When I was in my early teens my dad would drag us to Kentucky every chance he got. 10 hours each way it seemed to me most of our trip was driving. Finally, we would arrive at Aunt Lany's home, god I loved her . She had nine kids. My cousin Ronnie decided that he would tell us about an urban legend called the Devil lady of trace licking Hollow (or Holler as he liked to pronounce it).

Ronnie shared with us the following; Up on the outer ridge of this Hollow way above the tree line lived a bitter old woman who hated everyone and everything she was so full of hate that she started doing things to her neighbors. She took pets. When she would pass a neighbor on the road as they were walking beside the road she would try to take a swipe at them.

As this woman got older she started looking into people's windows scaring everyone but she would always disappear by the time any of the family would come out of their house. Then one family had had enough the father, grabbed his hunting rifle and made the hike up to the ridge where the old lady lived. When he entered her property something was not right it was too quiet. Then he saw her laying out in the middle of her small garden dead.

Dead for a very long time, how could she be still terrorizing the whole hillside. He also told me to stay away from the windows in the deepest part of night. I said ok , thinking this was just a ploy to get me to go to sleep and not get out of bed you see I'm a night owl my mother says I have been that way since I was in her womb.

So I walk upstairs and get into bed, and I cannot go to sleep so I start reading a book that I brought. The last chimes I remember were three. I turn over and look towards the window and I freeze there in the second floor bedroom window was this hideous face I have ever seen. Matted long hair, skin so thin that some was there and some just wasn't. Red eyes yellow teeth on the hag's head were horns. I was frozen I didn't know what to do I threw the blankets over my head and just kept praying the old hag would go away.

The next morning, I came down for breakfast and my aunt looked at me and said how did you sleep. I said ok I guess and when my aunt left the room my cousin Ronnie looks at me and says;
Buffy she always knows what's going on in her Holler.

THE SHADOW MAN

This all started when I was about 12, I'm 19 now. My sister (Zoey) father, step mother at the time, and her two daughters (Jade (my age) and Maddy, (my sisters age)) were camping. We had only been there for a day, and everything was fine. Then me and my sisters decided we were going to go to the stream by ourselves. My father gave us a walkie talkie so we could keep in contact while we were gone. Now the place we were going to was surrounded by bush, and to get there you had to go down a little path through it.

We spent a while with our shoes off and splashing in the water when jade said she could see someone standing in amongst the trees. We all looked and saw a figure. It was black but you could tell it was the shape of a man. You couldn't see the face. We stared for a few seconds and then he disappeared. We forgot about it and kept playing in the water. But I felt a little uneasy. A while later we all looked back wanting to know if he was still there. And he was. Everything was silent. I could hardly hear the rapids in the little stream. We stopped looking. After about 20 mins we headed back to the camp site.

My sisters lingered behind and I was about 20 meters ahead of them, but we couldn't see each other. I heard a twig snap behind me and I turned to look, assume they had caught up to me. Nope. I turned to see the tall dark black figure literally a foot behind me. So I started running.

The whole time I could feel him close behind. I ran as fast as I could, until I was out in the open camp ground. He was gone. My sisters came out not long after. And I told them what happened. I asked but none of them had seen him behind me, they were too far behind, and the path was windy so they were around a corner from me most of the time.

Throughout our camping trip we didn't see him around as much but occasionally would see him just standing there. Fast forward a couple years and we go back there. With my father's new girlfriend and her daughter, Stella. I can't recall this trip as much but I know for a fact that Stella saw him too.

Three years ago I started seeing him at my house. Just anywhere and everywhere really. One day I was out in the back yard, and I started to lean down to pat my cat when in my peripheral vision I saw him right behind me. I ignored him as he's never really done anything harmful really. Look solely at my cat as to block him out. As I do, I feel a hand grab my hair and tug. I immediately spun around. Nothing there. I dashed off inside as I was a bit spooked.

I now live with my boyfriend, and can't say 100% if I've seen it again. I sometimes see shadows move behind me in the reflection of the Tv but when I look behind me there's nothing so I just chalk it up to a trick of the light.

I did hear something recently. This is the most recent event I've had. My boyfriend's alarm went off for work, waking me up too. He switched it off but lay in bed a bit longer. I was awake then, facing my boyfriend's back, one eye closed as it was smooshed against the pillow. Suddenly, I hear someone whisper my name in my ear. It was so clear, and I could even feel cold breath on me. I sat up and said to my boyfriend "did you say my name?" He looked confused, he was just sitting there playing on his phone. "No" he said he hadn't. Which I believed. Because it was a female's voice. These two experiences don't match each other, but I really just don't understand them.

WHITLOCK'S LAKE MYSTERY

To understand why my mother and I were out at Whitlock Lake. My mother and I run a wreath business in a quiet Northern Michigan town. Violent crimes are virtually nonexistent. It was fall, around this time of year the forests in Michigan become rich with color. This day was full of warmth and color. Instead of buying pine cones for decorating wreaths, we decided to go foraging for them in our local woods.

I knew about Whitlock lake from my high school days. Some of my friends and I went out there a couple times to party. It's a small camping area with about 3 sites. This lake is connected to another bigger lake a few miles down the road. It is in a small old logging town called Jennings, pop. 20 maybe a little less or more. The times I went out there as a high school student it never had a strange feeling in the air. The day my mother and I went to forage, the air was thick with fear and we felt like we were being watched.

We thought maybe it was just a small woodland creature hiding and watching...waiting for us to leave so we continued. About an hour goes by and we decided to move on. We moved to where the forest meets the water. There are cute tiny little baby pine cones that we use for our table top wreaths. Shortly after we found ourselves at the edge of the lake, we heard a few gunshots from across the lake. We live in Northern Michigan people are getting ready for hunting season around this time of year so we shrugged it off.

We got into our car and moved down the trail. When we got out of my car, I noticed quite a few shotgun shells on the ground. Again, it's not uncommon to find shells of any sort on the ground this time of year, we continued. We were at the end of the trail with the last two campsites on either side of the trail. We continued foraging for about 20 more minutes. As we walked across the trail to the next site, we noticed something very strange.

At the opening of the campsite we noticed a tall 5ft or 6ft wooden pole. On top of that pole we saw two leather straps wafting in the wind. To us that was strange, why would someone want leather straps on a pole? Of course, we put it out of our minds and continued. A short while later we stumbled upon an old beat up mattress that looked like it had been there for a while now.

As we got closer to the mattress the ground around it was very mucky. As soon as you stepped somewhere you sunk about a half a foot down. People dump garbage in the woods a lot up here. When we started walking past it to get to the pine cones on the other side, this horrible smell seeped into our nostrils. We both looked at each other at the same time and got the hell out of there. By now we're scared out of our wits. As we were driving out of the trail-head, we were met by a guy in a red Cadillac type vehicle. The look on his face scared the bejesus out of us. Maybe it was a coincidence, maybe it was all in our heads. I would like to think that my mother and I have a good sense for that sort of thing and we got out of there just in the nick of time.

Needless to say, my mother and I have never been back to the lake and don't plan on going back. About a week later I couldn't hold this event inside myself anymore so I called the cops and recalled the incident as best as I could. They said they would look into it, and I haven't heard anything since. This happening still haunts me to this day. I'm always thinking about what may have actually happened out there.

CHASED BY A CRAZY CAT MASS MURDERER

When I was 16 years old I lived in rural area in England in a small village, if you could call it that, as it was nothing more than a bunch of houses with a small store. The closest school was the next town over and that was half an hour away so every morning I would have to get up at 6:00 am to catch the bus.

The bus wasn't that bad because of the 2 other kids who lived there who were close to my age Connor and Courtney (names have been changed) Courtney was the year below me and Connor was in my class. We got the bus together every morning and over the weekends and holidays we would hang out together at each other's houses or loiter around the shop until we got kicked out.

Anyway at the time I had a cat which I had gotten for my 15th birthday his name was King because he looked like a king. He was a huge white cat with green eyes and an attitude. I loved that cat so much so when he went missing I was pretty messed up and spent weeks crying my eyes out waiting for him to come home but he never did.

Soon it began going around that a lot of the neighbor's cats had been disappearing as well none of them had been found on the roads so people assumed that a fox had got them. It was the weekend and me, Connor and Courtney had decided that we were bored of hanging around Courtney's. So we decided to go exploring which meant that we would walk along the back roads until we were completely lost and then try and find our way back it was stupid but fun.

Anyway we were going up a back road we had never been up before when we came across a path way leading off the road it was unkempt and looked like nobody had used it for years. We went down the path excited to see where it led and we were even more excited when we found an old rundown house at the end of it.

The door was open and barely standing Connor carefully moved it aside and we went in. The smell was putrid and I'm pretty sure I retched a little. Everything was filthy and falling apart. Just being there gave me a weird sick feeling in my stomach something didn't feel right Courtney must have felt it too because she immediately began complaining that we should leave. I would have left if I hadn't been trying to impress Connor, who at the time I had a huge crush on, so instead of agreeing with her, Connor and I called her a sissy and teased her until she agreed to come with us through the rest of the house. We went through the what looked to be the living room it was covered in dirt and piles of trash the smell got worse as we made it to the bottom of the stairs Courtney made it clear that she didn't want to go up there but when we told her to wait for us there she made it even clearer that she didn't want to do that either.

So we all went up together, Courtney clinging to my arm and me clinging to Connor who went up first. At the top of the stairs there was a corridor with about 3 rooms it was just as filthy as downstairs and the smell was ten times worse. We piled in to the first room we came to pushing Connor in first only for him to freeze I looked over his shoulder and nearly puked the room was full of decomposing bodies of what looked to be cats all piled up against the wall the stench was horrendous.

I heard Connor whisper a swear word under his breath and I guess Courtney who was outside the room heard to because she loudly began asking what it was but before I could tell her to shut up from the Corner of the room came something flying through the air it hit Connor straight in the chest and fell to the floor it was a decaying cat corpse and it was followed by a deranged scream of "get out!!". And from out of the same corner stumbled a filthy old man he began to stagger towards us.

We immediately got the heck out of there and I don't remember much about it other than me and Courtney screaming out heads off and me tripping over one of the door frames on our way out we ran until we couldn't run anymore luckily we remembered our way back but it took us at least 30 minutes to get back home and in that time we speed walked as fast as we could jumping at every sound and of course on my part crying as I repeatedly asked him if he thought my cat was in there. Connor just kept replying that he didn't know and asking me if I thought the man had followed us.

We finally made it back and ran to the closest house which one of us lived in which was Courtney's and we hurriedly explained what happened and Courtney's mom called my mother, Connor's mother and then the police who came by a couple of hours later and took statements. Connor told me that they came back a few days later and said that the cats were there but there was no sign of the man. When I was visiting my mother earlier this month my boyfriend and I went to check out the house but it had been knocked down. I have no idea what that man was doing there that day or if he had killed the all the cats but I have a feeling that my cat was somewhere within those corpses and it still makes me sick to his day.

SKIN WALKER SIGHTING

On one particular hot summer weekend me and a couple friends including my boyfriend, let's call him Tony and my older brother let's call him Brad, decided we were going to go camping for the weekend since it was such a nice warm week. Tony's parents had owned a cabin way out in Ludington surrounded by a huge wooded area with a personal lake and no neighbors for at least 4 miles. But being stupid teenagers we didn't really think about that. All we were ready for was to party like any normal teens would. Well after being there for two hours our fun had started. Tony's friends had brought tons of alcohol to last us for the weekend so we wouldn't be bored since we had no service and only movies to watch.

After it got around 12 am and was pitch black we had a huge bonfire going, it was a total of six people including me and Tony. As we talked and laughed about upcoming events in our lives, we were so distracted that we didn't notice that my brother had literally frozen his eyes on to one section of the woods. Mind you we were all intoxicated and high at that time. Eventually our talking ceased when Tony realized his friend and my brother had an emotionless expression. "hey dude. You alright?" He asked Brad. Silence. Brad didn't reply or even make any movements that would indicate he heard him.

After that I started to get scared as well as the other two girls there. It took a lot for my brother to act that way. Eventually I was the first to catch on that he was excessively staring into a certain spot in the woods. I turned my head and followed his gaze the best I could. And when I finally caught on to what he was staring at my heart dropped. There right in front of us was (at first look) a dog. At least that's what I thought. It was some person's dog that wondered off. But then my Brain kicked in and I realized there wasn't neighbors for miles. So how could there be a dog? My mind started to race while Tony still tried to get brad to speak or even move.

In one motion this thing stood up tall. And when I say tall I mean gigantic. It had to be at least 6ft tall. Everyone seen it then. How could you not? The other two girls and the other boy with us gasped as they finally grasped why my brother was as still as a stick. No one moved for what seemed like hours. Tony was the first to talk "No tail" he mumbled. No one heard what he said but Brad. And I swear to you when I say his eyes widen as big as pan saucers. That freaked me out immediately. "What did you say?" One of the girls asked. "It. Has. No. Freaking. Tail" he hissed at her. My heart beat stopped. He was right. There was NO tail on this thing. Suddenly my clouded alcohol mind cleared up in a fraction of a second when I finally realized what this thing was.

Now I understood why my brother was basically pooing his pants. This thing was a Skinwalker. My instincts kicked in right then and there but before I could get the heck out of there the thing let off a terrible stench like rotting meat before screaming inhuman like. The sound was enough to scare everyone. My brother was the first up out of his chair, and started shouting native words to the creature why I told everyone to get the inside.

No one questioned me when they seen just how dead serious I was, especially Tony. He's never seen me so scared so he knew it was a bad situation. We all hi-tailed it into the cabin with my brother in tow still shouting native words at the creature which seemed to keep it at bay while it gave us enough time to get inside. He slammed and locked the door before turning all the lights off and grabbing a special ash from the kitchen counters and started throwing it at every window and door while chanting.

Of course he had everyone freaked out and basically in tears at that moment. After he was done no one said a word for a long time. All of us still in shock. He grabbed our dad's pistol and had it posted by him for hours. Everyone was entirely too shaken up to even questioned what happened. We must've fallen asleep eventually because I woke up to my brother packing all our stuff into the two cars early in the morning. I understood why. We had family. We knew what we were dealing with and we knew it would come back and maybe not alone. Before we left I did a blessing on the cabin and spoke a few calming words to the still very freaked out girls. We left as soon as everything was packed up.

To this day we still haven't explained exactly to our friends what happened that night. And they never bothered to ask us either...

CAMPING

JOKE BOOK

JOKES, PUNS, RIDDLES, & FUNNY STORIES
TO SNORT, LAUGH & GIGGLE

~ INTRODUCTION ~

GET READY FOR LAUGHTER

There's nothing better than seeing everyone in your campsite laugh or start a conversation leading into a rabbit hole of fun. Sometimes jokes can be annoying, but kids absolutely love them. Especially when they can see you get annoyed by them!

This book is broken into puns, short jokes, long jokes and funny stories. It's deigned to sit around the campfire and get a good chuckle from everyone. Make sure to share the book around so everyone can have a turn. But also the funny stories make for quiet time reading so you someone can curl up in chair and giggle to themselves. I'm confident you'll love the humor and your kids will be excited to get out the book and simply have a good time around the campfire.

Bill
Editor

~ PUNS ~

THE HIGHEST FORM OF WIT?

Did you hear about the guy whose whole left side was cut off? He's all right now.

Yesterday I accidentally swallowed some food coloring. The doctor says I'm OK, but I feel like I've dyed a little inside.

I wasn't originally going to get a brain transplant, but then I changed my mind.

I'd tell you a chemistry joke but I know I wouldn't get a reaction.

Why don't some couples go to the gym? Because some relationships don't work out.

I wondered why the baseball was getting bigger. Then it hit me

A friend of mine tried to annoy me with bird puns, but I soon realized that toucan play at that game.

Did you hear about the guy who got hit in the head with a can of soda? He was lucky it was a soft drink.

Have you ever tried to eat a clock? It's very time consuming.

The experienced carpenter really nailed it, but the new guy screwed everything up.

I'm reading a book about anti-gravity. It's impossible to put down.

When notes get in treble, bass-ically they get put behind bars. The alto-nate punishment is to push them off a clef and hope they land flat on sharp objects.

A man just assaulted me with milk, cream and butter. How dairy.

Why don't programmers like nature? It has too many bugs

If there was someone selling drugs in this place, weed know.
A prisoner's favorite punctuation mark is the period. It marks the end of his sentence.

I don't trust these stairs because they're always up to something.

I used to be a banker but I lost interest.

I like European food so I decided to Russia over there because I was Hungary. After Czech'ing the menu, I ordered Turkey. When I was Finnished I told the waiter 'Spain good but there is Norway I could eat another bite'.

The shoemaker did not deny his apprentice anything he needed. He gave his awl.

He drove his expensive car into a tree and found out how the Mercedes bends.

I relish the fact that you've mustard the strength to ketchup to me.

I don't know if I just got hit by freezing rain, but it hurt like hail.

Show me a piano falling down a mineshaft and I'll show you A-flat minor.

Claustrophobic people are more productive thinking outside the box.

When William joined the army he disliked the phrase 'fire at will'.

So what if I don't know what apocalypse means!? It's not the end of the world!

It's not that the man did not know how to juggle, he just didn't have the balls to do it.

I couldn't quite remember how to throw a boomerang, but eventually it came back to me.

I went to the dentist without lunch, and he gave me a plate.

The one who invented the door knocker got a No-bell prize.

It's a lengthy article on Japanese Sword Fighters but I can Samurais it for you.
Did you know they won't be making yard sticks any longer?
I'm glad I know sign language, it's pretty handy.

Police were called to a daycare where a three-year-old was resisting a rest.

What did the grape say when it got stepped on? Nothing - but it let out a little whine.

The roundest knight at king Arthur's round table was Sir Cumference.

A small boy swallowed some coins and was taken to a hospital. When his grandmother telephoned to ask how he was a nurse said 'No change yet'.

What is the difference between a nicely dressed man on a tricycle and a poorly dressed man on a bicycle? A tire.

A bicycle can't stand on its own because it is two-tired.

My friend's bakery burned down last night. Now his business is toast.

The other day I held the door open for a clown. I thought it was a nice jester.

I once heard a joke about amnesia, but I forgot how it goes.

I knew a woman who owned a taser, man was she stunning!

The girl quit her job at the doughnut factory because she was fed up with the hole business.

When Peter Pan punches, they Neverland.

Need an ark to save two of every animal? I noah guy.

There was once a cross-eyed teacher who couldn't control his pupils.

The first time I used an elevator it was really uplifting, then it let me down.

The man who survived mustard gas and pepper spray is now a seasoned veteran.

To write with a broken pencil is pointless.
Never discuss infinity with a mathematician, they can go on about it forever.

A new type of broom came out; it is sweeping the nation.

I used to have a fear of hurdles, but I got over it.

I once got into so much debt that I couldn't even afford my electricity bills, they were the darkest times of my life.

It was an emotional wedding. Even the cake was in tiers

Is old rope good enough for a hanging? Frayed knot. That stuff is bad noose. I did a theatrical performance about puns. Really it was just a play on words.

There was a sign on the lawn at a drug re-hab center that said 'Keep off the Grass'.

The butcher backed up into the meat grinder and got a little behind in his work.

I really wanted a camouflage shirt, but I couldn't find one.

I was going to buy a book on phobias, but I was afraid it wouldn't help me.

I think Santa has riverfront property in Brazil. All our presents came from Amazon this year.

I was going to look for my missing watch, but I could never find the time.

Two hats were hanging on a hat rack in the hallway. One hat says to the other, 'You stay here, I'll go on a head.

I saw a beaver movie last night; it was the best dam movie I've ever seen.

I don't get people who stumble into mirrors. They need to watch themselves.

What do you call a bald monster? A lock-less monster.

When the window fell into the incinerator, it was a pane in the ash to retrieve.

A quarter-acre of undeveloped land may not seem like much to some people, but to me it's a lot.

Smaller babies may be delivered by stork but the heavier ones need a crane.

I knew a guy who collected candy canes, they were all in mint condition.

I told my wife that it was her turn to shovel and salt the front steps. All I got was icy stares.

The dead batteries were given out free of charge.

When the cannibal showed up late to the luncheon, they gave him the cold shoulder.

There is a special species of bird that is really good at holding stuff together. They are called velcrows.

If towels could tell jokes they would probably have a dry sense of humor.

Alternative facts are aversion of the truth.

If you lose your hearing, is it ear replaceable?

What do dogs do after they finish obedience school? They get their masters.

Always trust a glue salesman. They tend to stick to their word.

What's the definition of a will? (It's a dead giveaway).

Two peanuts were walking in a tough neighborhood and one of them was a-salted.

My friend was fired from his job at the road department for stealing. I have to say I saw it coming. The last time I was at his house all the signs were there.

I used to be addicted to soap, but I'm clean now.

Why did the pig stop sunbathing? He was bacon in the heat.
Did you hear about the crime that happened in a parking garage? It was wrong on so many levels.

Whenever there is an earthquake the geologists are always quick to find fault.

The tale of the haunted refrigerator was chilling.

When a clock is hungry it goes back four seconds.

My new theory on inertia doesn't seem to be gaining momentum.

My fear of roses is a thorny issue. I'm not sure what it stems from, but it seems likely I'll be stuck with it.

The store keeps calling me to come back and buy more bedroom furniture, but all I really wanted was one-night stand.

Novice pirates make terrible singers because they can't hit the high seas.

Einstein developed a theory about space, and it was about time too.

What did the man say when the bridge fell on him? The suspension is killing me.

I would tell you a leech joke, but it would suck anyway.

Some people's noses and feet are built backwards: their feet smell and their noses run.

Broken puppets for sale. No strings attached.

Sleeping comes so naturally to me, I could do it with my eyes closed.

A hungry traveler stops at a monastery and is taken to the kitchens. A brother is frying chips. 'Are you the friar?' he asks. 'No. I'm the chip monk,' he replies.

I think I'm going to hire the same landscaper I used last year - he was really easy to get a lawn with.

What is a thesaurus' favorite dessert? Synonym buns.

I mixed up the cardiac resuscitation equipment with the lie detector, but I will de-fib you later.

My tailor is happy to make a pair of pants for me, or at least sew it seams.

Where do you imprison a skeleton? In a rib cage.

The Balloon family name died off when it ran out of heir.

The patron saint of poverty is St. Nickels.

I was going to tell you a joke about infinity, but it didn't have an ending.

How do trains drink? They chug.

When a female sheep turns around and goes the other way it makes a ewe turn.

My job at the concrete plant seems to get harder and harder.

There was a big paddle sale at the boat store. It was quite an oar deal.

A relief map shows where the restrooms are.

Proper punctuation can make the difference between a sentence that's well-written and a sentence that's, well, written.

I don't mind kids playing hopscotch in most places, but my driveway is where I draw the line.

I used to hate math but then I realized decimals have a point.

Weight loss pills stolen this morning - police say suspects are still at large.

I wrote a book about birds. It flew off the shelf.

Weight loss mantra? Fat chants!

My student was late for class, claiming he was in the washroom. I think he was stalling.

I try wearing tight jeans, but I can never pull it off.

Time flies like an arrow. Fruit flies like a banana.

Why would an hour glass only take half an hour to finish? It was filled with quick sand.

Children who fail their coloring exams always need a shoulder to crayon.

I was struggling to figure out how lightning works then it struck me.

People are choosing cremation over traditional burial. It shows that they are thinking out of the box.

Why did the capacitor kiss the diode? He just couldn't resistor.
There were two peanuts walking down a dark alley, one was assaulted.

What do you call a sleepwalking nun...
A roamin' Catholic.

How do you make holy water? You boil the hell out of it.

Why did the orange stop? Because, it ran outta juice.

What's brown and sounds like a bell? Dung!

Collection of Puns

Hickory Daiquiri:

One doctor always stopped at a local bar after work for a hazelnut daiquiri - a special drink the bartender created just for him. One day, the bartender ran out of hazelnut flavor so he substituted hickory nuts instead. The doctor took one sip of the drink and exclaimed, 'This isn't a hazelnut daiquiri!' 'No, I'm sorry', replied the bartender, 'it's a hickory daiquiri, doc.'

Too Tense:

A guy goes to a psychiatrist. 'Doc, I keep having these two dreams. First I'm a teepee; then I'm a wigwam; then I'm a teepee; then I'm a wigwam. It's driving me crazy. What's wrong with me?' The doctor replies: 'You gotta relax. You're two tents.'

Mathematics:

An Indian chief had three wives, all of which gave birth. The first had a boy and the chief built her a teepee of deer hide. The second also had a boy and the chief built her a teepee of antelope hide. When the third gave birth, the chief built her a two story teepee, made out of a hippopotamus hide. The chief then challenged the tribe to guess what had occurred. Many tried, unsuccessfully.

Finally, one young brave declared that the third wife had given birth to twin boys. 'Correct,' said the chief. 'How did you figure it out?'

The warrior answered, 'It's elementary. The value of the squaw of the hippopotamus is equal to the sons of the squaws of the other two hides.'

~ SHORT JOKES~
GET READY TO GIGGLE

What did the 0 say to the 8?
Nice belt!

Knock knock. Who's there? Interrupting Cow. Interrupting Cow wh-
MOOOOOOO!

Why did the storm trooper buy an iPhone?
He couldn't find the Droid he was looking for.

Why is six afraid of seven?
Because seven ate nine.

How many Alzheimer's patients does it take to change a light bulb?..... To
get to the other side!

What did one snowman say to the other?
Nice balls.

How do you make a tissue dance?
You put a little boogie in it.

Why did the policeman smell bad?
He was on duty.

Why does Snoop Dogg carry an umbrella?
FOR DRIZZLE!

What did the Zen Buddhist say to the hotdog vendor?
Make me one with everything.

What do you get when you cross an elephant and a rhino?
Elephino!

What did the farmer say when he couldn't find his tractor?
"Where's my Tractor?!"

Have you heard about the duck that was arrested for stealing?
He was selling "quack".

What do you call a cow with two legs?
Lean beef.

How do you catch a unique rabbit?

You 'neek' up on it.

What do you get when you cross an insomniac, an agnostic and a dyslexic?
Someone who lays awake at night wondering if there really is a dog.

What do you call a deer with no eyes?
No eye deer.

What's the last thing that goes through a bug's mind as he hits the
windshield?
His butt.

Knock knock- who's there? Dwayne. Dwayne who? Dwayne the tub I'm
dwouning!

The past, present and future walk into a bar. It was tense.

Why was Tiger looking in the toilet?
He was looking for Pooh!

What do you get when you throw a piano down a mine shaft?
A flat mine

Have you heard about the cannibal that passed his brother in the forest?

Who's there?" ... "Control freak. Okay now you say, 'Control freak who?"

Confucius says, when naked man walks through doorway sideways, he
going to Bangkok.

Horse walks into a bar. Bartender says, "Why the long face?"

A mushroom walks into a bar. The bartender says, "Hey, get out of here!
We don't serve mushrooms here". Mushroom says, "why not? I'm a fungi!"

I never make mistakes...I thought I did once; but I was wrong.

What's Beethoven's favorite fruit?...Ba-na-na-naaa!

How do you catch a tame rabbit?
The 'tame' way.

What did the green grape say to the purple grape?

BREATHE!

How many flies does it take to screw in a light bulb?
Two…. but I don't know how they got in there.

Why did the stop light turn red?
You would too if you had to change in the middle if the street!

Bacon and eggs walk into a bar and order a beer, the bartender says sorry,
we don't serve breakfast.

What do you do with a dead chemist?
You Barium.

If you're American in the living room, what are you in the bathroom?
European!

What does the man in the moon do when his hair gets too long?
Eclipse it!

What goes "ha ha thump"?
A man laughing his head off.

What's brown and sticky?
A stick!

Why did the stadium get hot after the game?
All of the fans left.

What did the duck say to the bartender?
Put it on my bill

What do you call a group of unorganized cats?
A Cat-astrophe

Why did the frog take the bus to work?
His car got toad.
Why did the dinosaur cross the road?
Because the chicken joke wasn't invented yet.

Why couldn't Dracula's wife get to sleep?
Because of his coffin.

What did the worker at the rubber band factory say when he lost his job?
Oh Snap!

What did the horse say when he fell?
Help, I've fallen and I can't giddy up!

What happens when the smog lifts over Los Angeles?
UCLA

Which U.S. State has the smallest soft drinks?
Mini-soda.

What did the buffalo say to his son when he left for college?
Bison

How do most frogs die?
They Kermit suicide!

Why did the elephants get kicked out of the public pool?
They kept dropping their trunks.
What's the most musical part of a chicken?
The drumstick.

Why did Johnny throw the clock out of the window?
Because he wanted to see time fly!
Why was the baby strawberry crying?
Because his mom and dad were in a jam.

What do lawyers wear to court?
Lawsuits!

Why did the man put his money in the freezer?
He wanted cold hard cash!

What do you call cheese that isn't yours?
Nacho Cheese

What's easy to get into but hard to get out of?
Trouble

What do you call two fat people having a chat?
A heavy discussion

What dog keeps the best time?
A watch dog

Why does a Moon-rock taste better than an Earth-rock?
Because it's a little meteor.

Why is Peter Pan always flying?
He neverlands!

Why did the picture go to jail?
Because it was framed!

How do you impress a baker when you're taking his daughter on a date?
Bring her flours.
Why did the yogurt go to the art exhibit?
Because it was cultured.

What do you call a fat psychic?
A four chin teller

What is the difference between a dressmaker and a farmer?
A dressmaker sews what she gathers, a farmer gathers what he sows.

What do you give to a sick lemon?
Lemon aid!

What do they call cans in Mexico?
Mexi-cans.

What do you get when you cross a snowman with a vampire?
Frostbite

What do you call an apology written in dots and dashes?
Remorse code.

Why couldn't the bicycle stand up by itself?
It was two-tired!

What is an astronaut's favorite place on a computer?
The Space bar!

Which month do soldiers hate most?
The month of March!

What runs but doesn't get anywhere?
A refrigerator

What do you call a guy who never farts in public?
A private tutor

Why did the hipster burn his tongue with his pizza?
He ate it before it was cool!

How do you get an astronaut baby to sleep?
Rocket

What should an astronaut do when he gets dirty?
Take a meteor shower

What did the astronaut get when the rocket fell on his foot?
Mistletoe.

What did the astronaut think of the restaurant on the moon?
He thought the food was fine but there wasn't much of an atmosphere.

What did the astronaut see on the stove?
An unidentified frying object.

What do you call an astronaut's watch?
A lunar-tick.

Where do astronauts keep their sandwiches?
In their launch boxes.

Why don't astronauts relate well to other people?
They are not always down-to-earth.

Why do astronauts wear bullet-proof vests?
To protect themselves against shooting stars.

What happens to astronauts who misbehave?
They're grounded.

Did you hear the one about the spaceship?
It was out of this world.

What do you call a space magician?
A flying saucerer.

What kind of Star Wars toy can you ride?
A Toy-Yoda.
When is the moon not hungry?
When it is full.

How did the rocket lose its job?
It was fired.

How does the astronaut describe his work?
Heavenly.

What do you get when you run in front of a car?
Tired

What do you get when you run behind a car?
Exhausted.

What did the fish say when it swam into a concrete wall? DAM
Two Eskimos sitting in a kayak were chilly, so they lit a fire in the craft.
Unsurprisingly it sank, proving once again that you can't have your kayak and
heat it too.

Two hydrogen atoms meet. One says 'I've lost my electron.'
The other says 'Are you sure?'
The first replies 'Yes, I'm positive.'

Did you hear about the Buddhist who refused Novocain during a root canal?
His goal: transcend dental medication.

Two boll weevils grew up in South Carolina. One went to Hollywood and
became a famous actor. The other stayed behind in the cotton fields and
never amounted to much. The second one, naturally, became known as the
lesser of two weevils.

A three-legged dog walks into a saloon in the Old West. He sidles up to the
bar and announces: "I'm looking for the man who shot my paw."

There was a man who entered a local paper's pun contest. He sent in ten
different puns, in the hope that at least one of the puns would win.
Unfortunately, no pun in ten did.

What's the difference between a bison and a buffalo?
You can't wash in a buffalo

There was three tomatoes walking down a street. The daddy tomato and the mammy tomato were way ahead of the baby tomato. The daddy tomato got so annoyed at the baby tomato for being so slow that he turned around real quickly and smacked his hands together and roared "KETCHUP" !!!!

A polar bear goes into a pub and says to the barman: "I'd like a......................packet of salt and vinegar crisps please." The barman replies, "Sure, but why the big pause?"

A three legged dog walk bursts into a wild west saloon and says
"I'm looking for the man who shot my paw"

A grasshopper walks into a bar. The bartender says "hey! we've got a drink named after you!". The grasshopper says "you have a drink named Murray?!"

A man buys two monkeys. those monkeys multiply and soon he's got 10 monkeys. the city gets wind of it and threatens heavy fines if he doesn't get rid of the monkeys. So the man calls his cousin pedro and offers him $50.00 to take the monkeys to the zoo. a couple of hours pass, pedro calls and asks for fifty MORE dollars! the man says "listen, i just gave you $50.00 to take them to the zoo". Pedro says "yes, but now they want to go to the movies!".

A guy is driving down the motorway, knitting. Obviously this is dangerous driving as the driver has no hands on the wheel, so before long the police are catching up with him. One police car drives up alongside the offending vehicle, and motions for him to open his window.

"Pull over!", the policeman shouts across. "No --- pair of socks!"

Who is a penguin's favourite relative.
His Aunt Artica!

Why was there a fish in the piano?
Because it was a piano tuna.

What do you get if you cross a bird a car and a dog?
A flying carpet

What is white and walks through the desert?
A herd of yoghurt

What's the difference between a tennis ball and the Prince of Wales?
One is thrown to the air and the other is heir to the throne.

A guy tries to enter a nightclub but is stopped at the door by the bouncer
who tells him that he can't get in without wearing a necktie. The guy goes
back to his car, looks around but can't find a tie. He sees a set of jumper leads
in the back so he puts them around his neck and ties a rough knot. He walks
back to the nightclub. When the bouncer sees him he looks him over and
says "OK you can go in but don't start anything"

Why did the fly do an old fashioned dance on the jam jar?
Because it said "twist to open

What do you get if you cross a snowman with a vampire?
Frostbite!

Where did Napoleon keep his armies?
In his sleevies.

How do you kill a circus?
Go for the juggler.

A square and a circle walk into a bar. The square says to the circle, "Your
round!"
A linguistics professor was lecturing to his class.
"In English," he said, "a double negative forms a positive. In some languages,
though, such as Russian, a double negative is still a negative. However, there
is no language wherein a double positive can form a negative. "A voice from
the back of the room piped up, "Yeah, right."
There's a sausage and an egg in a frying pan. The sausage turns to the egg and
says: "Gosh egg, it's really hot in here, isn't it?" The egg turns to the sausage
and says: "Oh my god! A talking sausage!!"

A guy phones the local hospital and yells "You've gotta send help! My wife's
in labour!" The nurse says, "Calm down. Is this her first child?" He replies,
"No! This is her husband!"

What did the policeman say to his belly?
You're under a vest!

Why did the chicken cross the playground?
To get to the other slide!!!
Why do deep sea divers jump out of the boat backwards when they want to

go into the water?
Because if they jumped forward, they would fall into the boat.

What do you tell a mathematician on a Saturday night ?
Don't drink and derive.

What did the orange say to the banana on the street corner?
"Hi"

What did batman say to robin before they got in the car? Robin, get in the car

How do you catch a rhino wearing a wool hat?
You kick it's back. Then let the rhino chase you around a lake until the rhino is hot and takes off the hat. Now you can catch it like a normal rhino.

Why is a tree better than a guard dog?
It has more bark!

A woman went to a seance and was successful in contacting her husband. Hi," he said," it's me. Everything's better... sky is bluer... grass is greener. Nothing to do but eat and sleep all day." "Oh, thank goodness. You did get to Heaven." "Heaven?. I'm a buffalo in Montana!"

What's gray on the inside and clear on the outside?
An elephant in a baggie!

What's green and likes snow?
Ski-weed

My dog minton ate all my shuttlecocks.....badminton

A man walks into a greengrocers and says "Can I have a hammer please?". The assistant says "Sorry this is a greengrocers." The man replies "That's O.K. I've got my bike outside."

What's yellow and always pints north? A magnetic banana!

Cows

What do you call a cow with 2 legs?
Lean Beef

What do you call a cow with no legs?

Ground Beef

Why did the cow cross the road?
It was the chicken's day off.

A totally black cow was standing in the middle of the road. A man was cruising around a corner with no headlights on, no dome light, no lights on at all. He slams on the brakes at just the right time to miss the cow. How did the guy see the cow?
It was daytime.

What day do cows dread?
Moo-nday

What does a cow get paid for her labor?
Mooney

Where does a cow go on vacation?
Moontana or Cowifornia

What is a cow's favorite rock band?
Mootley Crue

What type of car does an average cow drive?
A Moodel T or a Moostang

What kind of car does a rich cow drive?
A Cattelac.

What is a cow's favorite school subject?
Cowculus.

How does a cow keep track of her appointments?
She checks her COWander

What is an unusually stupid cow called?
A Mooron.

Where do the cows go on Saturday night?
To the Moovies.

Where do cows go when they get married?
On a honeyMOOn

What do you call a cow that works for a gardener?
A lawn MOOer.

Why do cows wear bells?
Because their horns don't work.

What do you get when you have a cow and a duck?
Milk and Quackers.

How did the cowboy count his cows?
With a COWculator.

What do you call a cow that doesn't give milk?
A Milk Dud.

What kind of milk comes from a forgetful cow?
Milk of Amnesia.

Do you know why the cow jumped over the moon?
The farmer had cold hands.

What do you call a cow that just had a calf?
De-CALF-enated.

What does a cow ride when his car is broken?
A COW-askai MOO-torcycle.

What did they play at the cow's birthday?
MOO-sical chairs.

Why did the farmer give his cow a pogo stick?
He wanted a milk shake.

How do you get a cow to stop charging?
Take away its credit card.

Two cows were standing in a field. The first says, 'Moooo'. The second says, 'Hey! I was just about to say the same thing.'

Two cows walk into a bar.
First cow says, "Hey, have you heard about all that mad cow disease going around?"
Second cow says, "Yeah I have, so what?"

First cow says, "Well, aren't you afraid you might catch it?"
Second cow says, "No, not me. I'm a duck!"

Elephants

Why do elephants paint their toenails red?
So they can hide in cherry trees.

Have you ever seen an elephant in a cherry tree? (they will say NO). Works, doesn't it?!

How do you know there have been elephants in the fridge?
There's footprints in the butter..

Why do elephants paint their ears yellow?
That's not paint, its butter.

Why do elephants paint their toenails red, blue, green, orange, yellow, and brown?
So they can hide in a bag of M&Ms.

How did the pygmie break his back?
He tried to carry a bag of M&Ms home from the store.

Why is it dangerous to walk in the jungle between 3 and 4 in the afternoon?
That's when the elephants jump out of the trees.

Why are pygmies so small?
They walked in the jungle between 3 and 4 in the afternoon.

How do you get an elephant on top of an oak tree?
Stand him on an acorn and wait fifty years.

What if you don't want to wait fifty years?
Parachute him from an airplane.

Why isn't it safe to climb oak trees between 1 and 2 in the afternoon?
Because that is when the elephants practice their parachute jumping.

Why are elephant's feet shaped that way?
To fit on lily pads.

Why isn't it safe to walk on the lily pads between 4 and 5 in the afternoon?
That's when the elephants are walking on the lily pads.

Why are frogs such good jumpers?
So they can walk on the lily pads between 4 and 5 in the afternoon.

How do you get two elephants in a pickup truck?
One in the cab, one in the back.

How do you get two mice in a pickup truck?
You can't ... it's full of elephants.

Why do ducks have flat feet?
From stomping out forest fires!

Why do elephants have flat feet?
From stomping out burning ducks!

What did Tarzan say when he saw a herd of elephants running through the jungle?
'Here come the elephants running through the jungle!'

Why did the elephants wear sunglasses?
So Tarzan wouldn't recognize them.

What did Tarzan say when he saw a herd of elephants running through the jungle?
Nothing. He didn't recognize them with their sunglasses on.

What did Tarzan say when he saw a herd of giraffes in the distance?
'Haha! You fooled me once with those disguises, but not this time!'

What is the difference between an elephant and a plum?
An elephant is grey.

What did Jane say when she saw a herd of elephants in the distance?
'Look! A herd of plums in the distance' (Jane is color blind)
Why do cub scouts run so fast in the forest at night?
To escape the elephants swinging through the trees.

What's that yucky stuff between the elephant's toes?
Slow cub scouts!

How can you tell if an elephant is under your bed?
The ceiling is very close!

How do you know if there's an elephant in bed?
He has a big 'E' on his pajamas jacket pocket.

How do you tell an elephant from a field mouse?
Try to pick it up, If you can't, it's either an elephant or a very overweight field mouse.

How can you tell if an elephant has been in the refrigerator?
Footprints in the Jell-O.

How can you tell if there are 2 elephants in the refrigerator?
You can't shut the door!

How do you get an elephant into the fridge?
1. Open door.
2. Insert elephant.
3. Close door.

How do you get a giraffe into the fridge?
1. Open door.
2. Remove elephant.
3. Insert giraffe.
4. Close door.
The lion, the king of the jungle, decided to have a party. He invited all the animals in the jungle, and they all came except one. Which one?
The giraffe, because he was still in the fridge.

How do you know Tarzan is in the fridge?
You can hear Tarzan scream OYOYOYOIYOIYOOOOOO

How do you get two Tarzans in the fridge?
You can't, silly. There is only one Tarzan!

How do you get 4 elephants into a Volkswagen?
2 in the front and 2 in the back.

How do you know if there are 4 elephants in your fridge?
There's a VW parked outside it.

What did the fifth elephant in the VW discover?
The sun roof.

Why are there so many elephants running around free in the jungle?

The fridge isn't large enough to hold them all.

How do you get an elephant out of the water?
Wet.
How do you get two elephants out of the water?
One by one.

How do you shoot a blue elephant?
With a blue elephant gun, of course.

How do you shoot a yellow elephant?
There's no such thing as yellow elephants.

Why did the elephant fall out of the tree?
Because it was dead.

Why did the second elephant fall out of the tree?
It was glued to the first one.

Why did the third elephant fall out of the tree?
It thought it was a game.

And why did the tree fall down?
It thought it was an elephant.

Why do elephants wear sandals?
So that they don't sink in the sand.

Why do ostriches stick their head in the ground?
To look for the elephants who forgot to wear their sandals.

What did the elephant say when he saw a dead ant on the road?
Deadant, Deadant, Deadant! (sung to Pink Panther tune).

What did the elephant say when he saw a live ant on the road?
A: He stomped on it and then said 'Deadant, Deadant, Deadant!'.

Why did the elephant stand on the marshmallow?
He didn't want to sink in the hot chocolate.
How do elephants keep in touch over long distances?
They make trunk calls.

What's red and white on the outside and gray and white on the inside?

Campbell's Cream of Elephant soup.

How do you smuggle an elephant across the border?
Put a slice of bread on each side, and call him 'lunch'.

Why are elephants wrinkled?
Have you ever tried to iron one?

Why did the elephant cross the road?
Chicken's day off.

What do you call two elephants on a bicycle?
Optimistic!

What do you get if you take an elephant into the city?
Free Parking.

What do you get if you take an elephant into work?
Sole use of the elevator.

How do you know if there is an elephant in the bar?
It's bike is outside.

How do you know if there are three elephants in the bar?
Stand on the bike and have a look in the window.

Why do elephants wear tiny green hats?
To sneak across a pool table without being seen.
How many elephants does it take to change a light bulb?
Don't be stupid, elephants can't change light bulbs.

What do you get if you cross an elephant with a whale?
A submarine with a built-in snorkel.

How do you make a dead elephant float?
Well, you take 10 dead elephants, 10 tons of chocolate ice-cream, 5 tons of
bananas,.....

What do you know when you see three elephants walking down the street
wearing pink sweatshirts?
They're all on the same team.

How do you stop an elephant from charging?

Take away his credit card.

Why do elephants have trunks?
Because they would look silly with glove compartments.

What do you give a seasick elephant?
Lots of room.

What has two tails, two trunks and five feet?
An elephant with spare parts

What's grey and puts out forest fires?
Smokey the Elephant.

What happens when an elephant sits in front of you at the movies?
You miss most of the picture!

What did the peanut say to the elephant?
Nothing, peanuts can't talk.

How do you know when an Elephant has been in the baby carriage?
By the footprints on the baby's forehead!
What is beautiful, gray and wears glass slippers?
Cinderelephant.

What time is it when an elephant sits on your fence?
6:15PM (trick question!)

How do you shoot a blue elephant?
With a blue elephant gun.

How do you shoot a white elephant?
Hold his nose until he turns blue, then shoot him with a blue elephant gun.

Frogs

Why are frogs so happy?
They eat whatever bugs them!

What does a frog wear on St. Patrick's day?
Nothing!

What did the frog dress up as on Halloween?
A prince.

What car does a frog drive?
A Beetle.
What's green and jumps?
A frog!

What's green and red?
A very mad frog.

What's green with red spots?
A frog with the chicken pox!

What's green with bumps?
A frog with the measles!

What's black and white and green?
A frog sitting on a newspaper.

What's green and dangerous?
A frog with a hand-grenade.
What's white on the outside, and green on the inside?
A frog sandwich!

What do you say to a hitch-hiking frog?
Hop in!

What kind of shoes do frogs wear?
Open toad!

What do frogs do with paper?
Rip-it!

What happened to the frog's car when his parking meter expired?
It got toad!!

What do you call a frog that crosses the road, jumps in a puddle, and crosses
the road again?
A dirty double-crosser!

What is a frog's favorite time?
Leap Year!

Why did the frog walk across the road?
He didn't... he jumped.

Why did the frog cross the road?
To see what the chicken was doing.

Why did the frog cross the road?
Some mean little kid super-glued it to the chicken.

How can you tell if a frog is deaf?
You yell 'Free Flies' and he doesn't come.

What do you call a frog with no legs?
It doesn't matter- he won't come anyway.

What do you call a frog with legs?
Dinner.

Why did the frog croak?
Because he ate a poisonous fly!
What is a frog's favorite game?
Croquette.

What did the frog order at McDonald's?
French flies and a diet Croak.

What happened to the cat and frog when they got run over?
The cat still had eight lives, the frog just croaked.

Why did the frog say meow?
He was learning a foreign language.

What do you get if you add milk?
Frog nog!

What happens if you drink frog nog?
You Croak!

Why did the motorcycle rider buy a pet frog?
To pick the flies out from between his teeth!

What has more lives that a cat?
A frog - he croaks every night.

Why did the frog go to the bank with a gun?
He was going to robbit.

Why are frogs such liars?
Because they are amFIBians.

Top 10 Reasons Why It's Great Being a Frog
- Babes are always kissing you because they think you'll turn into a prince.
- Flies in your soup are a bonus.
- You're above toads on the food chain.
- Green goes with absolutely everything!
- Pond Scum is a term of endearment.
- Most restaurants have a 'no croaking' section.
- Amphibians are at a minimum risk of appearing on Geraldo.
- You can scratch hard to reach places with your tongue.
- You can donate your body to science for big bucks!
- It sure beats being a newt.

Mosquitos

What is the most religious insect?
A mosque-ito!

What flies, bites, and talks in code?
A morse-quito!

What do you get if you cross the Lone Ranger with an insect?
The Masked-quito!

What has antlers and sucks blood?
A moose-quito!

What is the difference between a mosquito and a fly?
You can't zip your mosquito!

What is a mosquito's favorite sport?
Skin-diving!

Why are mosquitos religious?
They prey on you!

Why did the mosquito go to the dentist?
To improve his bite!
Knock Knock
Who's there?
Amos.
Amos who?
A mosquito.

Knock Knock
Who's there?
Ann.
Ann who?
Another mosquito.

Knock Knock
Who's there?
Omar.
Omar who?
Omar Goodness - tons of mosquitos!

Halloween

What do zombies serve at tea?
Lady fingers.

What is the one thing that can harm Super-Mummy?
Crypt-onite

What do ghosts need before they can scare people?
A Haunting license.

Why did the Invisible Man forfeit the boxing match?
Because he was a no-show.

Why did the mummy miss the party?
Because she was all wrapped up in her work.

Why did the ghoul bury the trophy?
Because she wanted it engraved.

How did the corpse get out of the coffin?
It wormed its way free.

What position did the ghost play in the baseball game?
Fright Field

Why was the archeologist crying?
Because he wanted his Mummy.

What kind of a ship does a vampire sail?
A blood vessel.

What do you call a magic competition among witches?
A spelling bee.

What has fur, howls at the moon, and is easy to clean?
A Wash-and-Werewolf.

Who do monsters buy their cookies from?
The Ghoul Scouts.

Why aren't ghosts allowed in beauty parlors?
Because they're too hair-raising.

Where do monsters swim?
In Lake Eerie.

What did the ghost's mother say to her son on Halloween night?
You be scareful out there tonight.

Why couldn't Frankenstein dance?
He had two left feet.

What did the ghouls eat at the barbecue?
Handburgers and hot dogs.

What do grave robbers wear in the rain?
Ghoul-oshes.

What do you say to a ghost with three heads?
Hello, Hello, Hello.

What did the little boy ghost eat for lunch?
Booloney sandwich.

On which kind of street do ghosts live?

A Dead End

Who does a ghost love?
His ghoul friend.

What do you call a witch in poison ivy?
An Itchy Witchy

Who are the werewolves' relatives?
The Whatwolves and the Whenwolves.

What kind of pet does Dracula have?
A blood hound.

What kind of hotdogs to ghosts like best?
Halloweiners.
What do you call serious rocks?
Grave Stones.

Why did the witch stand up in front of the audience?
To give a Screech.

Why did the vampire stop working for 15 minutes?
It was his coffin break.

Why did Frankenstein's mail rattle?
It was a chain letter

Why did the vampire get heartburn at lunch?

He ate a steak sandwich
What instrument does a skeleton play in the band?
A tromBONE.

What is a vampire's favorite holiday?
FANGSgiving.

Ghosts

Where do baby ghosts go during the day?
Dayscare centers.

What monster flies his kite in a rain storm?
Benjamin Frankenstein.

121

What do ghosts serve for dessert?
Ice Scream.

What's a monster's favorite play?
Romeo and Ghouliet.
What do witches put on their hair?
Scare spray.

What do you get when you cross Bambi with a ghost?
Bamboo.
What's a haunted chicken?
A poultry-geist.
How can you tell when you're in bed with Count Dracula?
He has a big D on his pajamas.

What's pink and gray and wrinkly and old and belongs to Grandpa monster?
Grandma monster

What kind of mistakes do spooks make?
Boo boos.

Why do mummies make excellent spies?
They're good at keeping things under wraps.

What kind of cereal do monsters eat?
Ghost-Toasties.

What kind of monster is safe to put in the washing machine?
A wash and wear wolf.

What's the first thing ghosts do when they get into a car?
They boo-kle their seatbelts.

What has webbed feet, feathers, fangs and goes quack-quack?
Count Duckula.
Why are monsters huge and hairy and ugly?
Because if they were small and round and smooth they'd be M&Ms.

Why wasn't there any food left after the monster party?
Because everyone was a goblin!

How did the ghost patch his sheet?

With a pumpkin patch.

What do the birds sing on Halloween?
Twick or Tweet.

What did the little ghost have in his rock collection?
Tombstones.

Why should a skeleton drink 10 glasses of milk a day?
It's good for the bones.

What do baby ghosts wear on Halloween?
White Pillowcases.

What do you get when you drop a pumpkin?
Squash.

Why did the witches' team lose the baseball game?
Their bats flew away.

What was the witches favorite subject in school?
Spelling.

What does a vampire fear most?
Tooth decay.

Where did the vampire open his savings account?
At a blood bank.

Where do mummies go for a swim?
To the dead sea.

Where does Dracula water ski?
On Lake Erie.

What kind of boat pulls Dracula when he water skis?
A blood vessel.

What do you get when you divide the circumference of a jack-o-lantern by its diameter?
Pumpkin Pi.

Why are there fences around cemeteries?

Because people are dying to get in.

Why didn't the skeleton cross the road?
He didn't have the guts.
How does the silly witch know what time it is?
She looks at her witch-watch.

What did the Mommy ghost say to the baby ghost?
Don't spook until your spooken to.

Why do ghouls and demons hang out together?
Because demons are a ghoul's best friend!

Why don't witches like to ride their brooms when they're angry?
They're afraid of flying off the handle!

Relatives of Van Gogh

Researchers have recently discovered that the artist Vincent Van Gogh had quite a few interesting relatives.

A grandfather that moved to Yugoslavia: U Gogh

A dizzy blonde aunt: Verti Gogh

A brother that worked at a convenience store: Stopen Gogh

A magician uncle: Wherediddy Gogh

A psychiatrist nephew: E. Gogh

A niece that danced in a mini-skirt: Go Gogh

A very obnoxious brother: Please Gogh

A sister with a small bladder: Gotta Gogh

A cousin that moved to Illinois: Chica Gogh

A niece that moved to Mexico: Ami Gogh

A second cousin that drove a stagecoach: Wells Far Gogh

A birdwatching uncle: Flamin Gogh

A grand-niece that no one has heard from because she's been traveling around the USA for years: Winnie Bay Gogh

Chicken Crossing The Road

Why did the chicken run across the road?
There was a car coming.

Why did the chicken cross the road halfway?
She wanted to lay it on the line.

Why did the rubber chicken cross the road?
She wanted to stretch her legs.

Why did the chicken cross the road?
To prove to the possum, it could actually be done!

Why did the chicken cross the road twice?
Because it was a double-crosser

Why did the Roman chicken cross?
She was afraid someone would Caesar!

How did the wealthy rubber chicken cross the road?
In her Cadillac stretch limo.

Why did the turtle cross the road?
To get to the Shell station.

Why did the chicken scientist cross the road?
To invent the other side.

Why did the chicken lawyer cross the road?
To corrupt the other side.

Why did the chicken IRS representative cross the road?
To bankrupt the other side.

Why did the chicken lawyer cross the road?
To get to the car accident on the other side.

Why did chicken Jim Morrison cross the road?
To break on through to the other side
Why did the chicken cross the road?

Don't ask me, ask the chicken!

Why did the sheep cross the road?
To get to the Baa Baa Shop for a haircut

Why did the cow cross the road?
To get to the udder side

Why did the fish cross the road?
To get to its school

Why did the fish cross the ocean?
To get to the other tide!

Why didn't the skeleton cross the road?
Because he didn't have the guts

Why did the horse cross the road?
To reach his Nay-borhood.

Why did the rooster cross the road?
To prove he wasn't a chicken

Why did the dog cross the road?
To get to the barking lot

Why did the chicken stop crossing the road?
It got tired of everyone making so many jokes!

Books Never Written

'Under the Grand Stands' by Seymor Buts
'To the Outhouse' by Willie Maket, illustrated by Betty Wont
'How to Survive a Bear Attack' by Ben Eaton
'Walking to School' by Misty Bus
'How to Check a Pulse' by Izzy Dead
'Where Have All the Animals Gone?' by Darin Dabarn
'The Yellow River' by I.P. Daily
'Over the Mountaintop' by Hugo First
'The Numbers Game' by Cal Q. Later
'Rusty Bed Springs' by I.P. Freeley
'Falling Off a Cliff' by Eileen Dover
'The Joys of Drinking' by Al Coholic
'My Life with Igor' by Frank N. Stein
'Supporting Athletes' by Jacques Strappe
'I Was Prepared' by Justin Case
'Green Spots on the Wall' by Picken and Flicken
'Caulking Made Easy' by Phil McKrevis
'The Future of Robotics' by Cy Borg and Anne Droid
'What to Do if You're in a Car Accident' by Rhea Ender
'Breathing Lessons' by Hal E. Tosis
'Why Should I Walk?' by Iona Carr
'Deep in Debt' by Owen A. Lott
'Taking Tests' by B.A. Wiseman
'Pie' by Don Cherry
'Computer Memory' by Meg A. Byte
'Gotta Go' by C. U. Later
'How to Serve Your Fellow Man' by The Cannibals
'The Membership List' by Ross Terr
'The Giant Clock Tower' by 'Big' Ben
'All About Flowers' by Chris Anthymum
'Boy Scout Brigade' by Pat Troll
'The Lost Scout' by Werram Eye
'Late for Work' by Dr. Wages
'Ten Years in the Bathtub' by Rink Lee Prune
'How to Eat Cereal' by Poor A. Bowl
'Smelly Stuff' by Anita Bath
'Technology in the 21st Century' by Rob Ott
'A Safe Hitchiker's Guide' by Ren Tacar
'Things Women Can't Do' by B. A. Mann
'The Art of Being Discreet' by Anonymous
'Bubbles in the Bath' by Ivor Windybottom
'Microsoft Business Practices' by Eve Hill

'Gotta Go Again' by D. I. Aria
'Interesting Places Around the World' by Ben There & Don That
'101 Ways To Die' by Sue I. Cide
'Household Book of Tools' by M.C. Hammer
'Paris Monuments' by I. Phil Taurer
'The Bearded Chinaman' by Harry Chin
'How to Exercise' by Eileen and Ben Dover
'Magical Bed Wettings' by Peter Pants
'101 Ways to Diet' by I. M. Hungry
'Getting Fired' by Anita Job
'Great Restaurants' by Bo Leamick
'Crossing a Man with a Duck' by Willie Waddle
'A Sailor's Adventure' by Ron A. Ground
'Green Vegetables' by Brock Ali
'Raise Your Arms' by Harry Pitt
'Long Walk Home' by Miss. D. Bus
'Sitting on the Beach' by Sandy Cheeks
'Window Coverings' by Kurt and Rod
'Wheels in China' by Rick Shaw
'How To Dance' by Sheik Yerbouti
'Something Smells' by I. Ben Pharting
'I.Q. Competitions' by Samar T. Pants
'Depressing Jobs' by Paul Bearer
'The Skyline' by Bill Ding
'My Life as a Gas Station Attendant' by Phil R. Awp

~ LONG JOKES~
CAMPFIRE GREATS

Talking Dog

Three racehorses were in the stable waiting for the big race. Trying to psych each other out, they began bragging.

First horse, 'I've been in 38 races and have only lost twice.'

Second horse, 'Well, I've been in 47 races and have never lost.'

Third horse, 'Huh, I've never lost either and I even beat Secretariat twice.'

Just then, they heard a chuckle by the stable door, and there was a greyhound dog walking up to them.

The greyhound said, 'That's nothing. I've been in over 200 races and have won every one by at least 3 lengths.'

First horse, 'Wow! That's amazing - a talking dog!'

Art Thief

An art thief once stole some very expensive paintings from the Louvre in Paris. He took two Van Goghs, a couple Monets, a DeGas, and some other paintings.

Everything went perfectly, except he was captured sitting in his van with the paintings only two blocks from the museum. His van had run out of fuel!

When asked by the police how he could plan such a successful robbery and then be foiled by such a simple error, he replied...

'I had no MONET to buy DEGAS to make the VAN GOGH!'

Atoms Joke

Two atoms were walking down the sidewalk and suddenly one slips off the curb and says "Oh no, I've lost my electron!"

The other atom says "Are you sure?"

1st atom says "Yes, I'm positive!"

Bach Decomposing

Two grave robbers decided to rob a grave, that's what they do. They find a prety nice grave and start digging.

After they dug up the topsoil they found a hole and in the hole there was a man with wild white hair sitting in front of a piano. The man would play a couple notes then erase something on a piece of music.

The two men, amazed beyond belief, yelled down to the man, 'Who are you, and what are you doing?' The man looked up and said...

'IM BACH, AND IM DECOMPOSING'

Vampire Bat

Two vampire bats wake up in the middle of the night, thirsty for blood. One says, "Let's fly out of the cave and get some blood."

"We're new here," says the second one. "It's dark out, and we don't know where to look. We'd better wait until the other bats go with us."

The first bat replies, "Who needs them? I can find some blood somewhere." He flies out of the cave.

When he returns, he is covered with blood.

The second bat says excitedly, "Where did you get the blood?"

The first bat takes his buddy to the mouth of the cave. Pointing into the night, he asks, "See that black building over there?"

"Yes," the other bat answers.

"Well," says the first bat, "I didn't."

Beethoven's Ninth

The Boston Symphony recently performed Beethoven's Ninth symphony which is a wonderful piece that has a part near the end in which the bass violins do nothing. So, the bassists snuck offstage, out the backdoor, and next door to the local pub for a drink.

After quickly gulping down a few stiff drinks, one of them checked his watch and said, 'Oh no, we only have 30 seconds to get back!'

Another bassist said, 'Don't worry, I tied the last page of the conductor's score down with string to give us a bit more time. We'll be fine.'

So, they staggered and stumbled back into the concert hall and took their places just as the conductor was busily working on the knot in the string so he could finish the symphony.

Someone in the audience asked his companion, 'What's going on? Is there a problem?'

His companion said, 'This is a critical point - it's the bottom of the Ninth, the score's tied, and the bassists are loaded!'

Blind Pilots

Two men dressed in pilots' uniforms walk up the aisle of the aircraft. Both are wearing dark glasses, one is using a guide dog, and the other is tapping his way along the aisle with a cane.

Nervous laughter spreads through the cabin, but the men enter the cockpit the door closes, and the engines start up. The passengers begin glancing nervously around, searching for some kind of a sign that this is just a little practical joke. None is forthcoming.

The plane moves faster and faster down the runway, and the people sitting in the window seats realize they're headed straight for the water at the edge of the airport property. Just as it begins to look as though the plane will plow straight into the water, panicked screams fill the cabin.

At that moment, the plane lifts smoothly into the air. The passengers relax and laugh a little sheepishly, and soon all retreat into their magazines and books, secure in the knowledge that the plane is in good hands.

Meanwhile, in the cockpit, one of the blind pilots turns to the other and says, 'You know, Bob, one of these days, they're gonna scream too late and we're all gonna die'!!

Cheap Parking

In New York, a guy walks into a bank. He tells the loan officer that he needs to borrow $5000 because he is going to Europe for a two-week trip. The loan officer says the bank will need collateral for the loan so the guy hands him the keys and the title papers to his brand new Ferrari that is parked in the street in front of the bank.

Obviously, a $250,000 Ferrari is more than enough collateral so the loan officer gives him the $5000. The guy leaves and the loan officer drives the Ferrari into the bank's underground parking garage and parks it.

Over the next few days, the big joke among the bank employees is all about the foolish man that put up $250,000 collateral for a measly $5000 loan.

But, two weeks later, the guy returns from his trip and repays his loan. Plus $26.92 interest.

The loan officer says to the guy, "I want to thank you for your business, but I'm curious. While you were away, I checked and found out you are a multimillionaire. I don't understand why you bothered to borrow $5000 when you have so much money."

The guy replies, "Where else in New York can I park my Ferrari for $2.00/day and expect it to be there when I return?"

Chess Nuts

A chess tournament was in being held and contestants from around the world were in the lobby of the hotel bragging about other tournaments they had won. After a while, the hotel manager came out of the office and asked them to please leave.

'But why?' they asked, as they moved off.

'Because', he said, 'I can't stand chess-nuts boasting in an open foyer.'

Twins

A woman has twins and gives them up for adoption. One of them goes to a family in Egypt and is named 'Ahmal' while the other goes to a family in Spain and they name him 'Juan.'

Years later, Juan sends a picture of himself to his birth mother. Upon receiving the picture, she tells her husband that she wishes she also had a picture of Ahmal.

Her husband responds, 'They're twins! If you've seen Juan, you've seen Ahmal.'

Florist Friars

A group of friars from the monastery opened a florist shop to raise funds. A rival florist saw his business drop significantly. He asked the good fathers to close down, but they would not. He went back and begged the friars to close. They ignored him. So, the rival florist hired Hugh O'Reilly, the toughest thug in town to convince the friars to close down. Hugh beat up the friars and ruined their flowers, saying he'd be back if they didn't close up shop. Terrified, they did so, proving that 'only Hugh can prevent florist friars'.

Mahatma Gandhi

Mahatma Gandhi, as you know, walked barefoot most of his life, which produced an impressive set of calluses on his feet. He also ate very little, which made him rather frail. And with his odd diet, he suffered from bad breath. This made him:
A super calloused fragile mystic hexed by halitosis.

Writers

An author and one of his fans were in Africa on safari. One night as they sat around the campfire, the author working on a story and the fan reading the latest publication, a lion leapt into the camp. He jumped over the author, snatched the fan and carried him off into the brush.
Another on the safari looked at the author, "Why did he jump you and take your fan?" "That's a smart lion," said the author. "He knows that writers block, but readers digest."

Ropes

A rope walks into a bar. "We don't serve ropes in here", says the bartender. "You have to leave"
The rope goes out to the parking lot and considers a few moments. He fluffs his ends and twists around himself a few times, then shuffles back into the bar.
"Aren't you that rope I just kicked out?" asks the bartender.

"Nope, I'm a frayed knot."

Dog Fight

There were two countries, Blitzvia and Blatzvia, that were constantly at war. They fought year after year with neither side gaining an advantage. Finally, the leaders of both sides met and decided to have a contest to determine the victor before both countries were completely destroyed.

They decided to have a dog fight and whichever dog won, that country would rule both lands. Each country would have 7 years to breed the best fighting dog they could.

Seven years later, it was time for the fight. The Blitzvians had cross-bred Rottweilers, Wolfhounds, Dobermann's and Pit Bulls. They took the largest of each litter and breeded those again. They made the dogs fight for raw meat laced with steroids and stimulants and had to keep them in separate cages with strong steel bars. Three trainers were killed by the dogs during training. Finally, there was only one dog left - the biggest, meanest, nastiest dog ever.

When the Blitzvians arrived at the location chosen for the fight, the Blatzvians arrived pulling a trailer with a 10-foot-long Dachsund weiner dog riding on it, wagging its tail. The Blitzvians could hardly contain their laughter.

As soon as the two dogs were let loose in the ring, the killer dog charged the dachsund. But, the dachsund just opened its mouth unbelievably wide and swallowed the dog in one gulp. The fight was over and the Blatzvians had won!

The Blitzvians were stunned. They asked, 'Our best scientists, trainers, and drug experts spent 7 years breeding the mightiest of dogs. How did you defeat us?'

'Well, we had our best plastic surgeons spend 7 years making an alligator look like a dachsund.'

Firetruck Brakes

A fire started on some grassland near a farm. The county fire department was called to put out the fire. The fire was more than the county fire department could handle. Someone suggested that a nearby volunteer bunch be called.

Despite some doubt that the volunteer outfit would be of any assistance, the call was made.

The volunteers arrived in a dilapidated old fire truck. They rumbled straight towards the fire, drove right into the middle of the flames and stopped! The firemen jumped off the truck and frantically started spraying water in all directions. Soon they had snuffed out the center of the fire, breaking the blaze into two easily controlled parts.

Watching all this, the farmer was so impressed with the volunteer fire department's work and was so grateful that his farm had been spared, that right there on the spot he presented the volunteers with a check for $1,000. A local news reporter asked the volunteer fire captain what the department planned to do with the funds.

'That ought to be obvious,' he responded, wiping ashes off his coat. 'The first thing we're gonna do is get the brakes fixed on our fire truck!'

Frogs

A boy was crossing a road one day when a frog called out to him and said, 'If you kiss me, I'll turn into a beautiful Princess.' The boy picked up the frog and put it in his pocket.

The frog said, 'Hey, if you kiss me and turn me back into a beautiful Princess, I'll love you forever.' The boy took the frog out of his pocket, smiled at it, and put it back in his pocket.

The frog yelled, 'If you kiss me and turn me back into a Princess, I'll clean your house, cook for you, and love you forever.' The boy took the frog out, smiled at it, and put it back.

Finally, the frog asked, 'What is it? I've told you I'm a beautiful Princess, that I'll cook and clean for you and love you forever. Why won't you kiss me?'

The boy said, 'Look, I'm a cub scout. I don't have time for girlfriends, but a talking frog is really cool.

The librarian is working away when a chicken enters the library and walks up to her desk. The chicken clucks, 'Book, book, book, BOOK!'

The librarian sets a pile of four books in front of the chicken. The chicken grabs them and disappears out the front door.

About an hour later, the librarian sees the same chicken come into the library. It sets the four books down on the desk and again squawks, 'Book, book, book, BOOK!'

The librarian wonders what the chicken is doing with these books, but since they seem to be in fine shape, she takes the returns and gives the chicken 4 more books. The chicken zips out the door and down the road.

Another hour passes and the librarian hears a loud 'Book, book, book, BOOK!' She looks up from her work and sees the chicken back yet again! By now, the librarian's curiosity has gotten the better of her. She gives the chicken four more books and it heads for the door. This time, as soon as the chicken is gone, the librarian jumps up and runs to the door. She follows the chicken down the road for a half mile to an old farm. The chicken ducks through the fence and disappears into a cluster of trees.

The librarian hops the fence, and sneaks up to the trees. As she moves some branches aside, she sees the chicken standing by a pond handing each book to a frog. As the frog looks at the cover of each book, he says, 'Read It. Read It. Read It. ...'

Two frogs sitting on a lily pad when a fly came buzzing by. One frog put out his tongue, ate the fly, and started laughing. Soon the other frog joined in the laughter.

Then the other frog ate a fly and the two frogs burst out in laughter. As time went on, the frogs enjoyed the flies so much they nearly fell off their lily pad laughing.

A third frog hopped up to the first two and asked what was so funny. The first frog answered 'Time.'

'Huh?' asked the third frog.

The second frog explained: 'Time's fun when you're having flies.'

More Frogs

Once upon a time, there was a little green frog who had a very big mouth.

The frog was hopping down the road when he met a cat. He looked at the cat and then shouted, 'CAT! WHAT DO YOU EAT?'

The cat replied, 'I drink milk,' and returned to cleaning its whiskers.

The little frog said, 'OH! THAT'S NICE!' and continued down the road.

Then he met a dog. 'DOG!' shouted the frog, 'WHAT DO YOU EAT?'

The dog said, 'I eat meat.'

The frog shouted, 'OH! THAT'S NICE!' and continued down the road.

He met a cow grazing along the road and, even though the answer was obvious, the big-mouthed frog shouted, 'COW! WHAT DO YOU EAT?'

The cow blinked and said, 'Why, I eat grass, obviously.'

The frog shouted happily, 'OH! THAT'S NICE!' and continued down the road.

He found a large snake coiled in the center of the road and shouted, 'SNAKE! WHAT DO YOU EAT?'

The snake hissed and looked at him before replying, 'I eat little frogs with big mouths.'

The frog blinked, then whispered in a very small voice, 'Oh... that's nice.'

Frogs can Jump

A scientist was interested in studying how far bullfrogs can jump. He brought a bullfrog into his laboratory, set it down, and commanded, 'Jump, frog, jump!'

The frog jumped.

The scientist measured the distance, then noted in his journal, 'Frog with four legs jumped six feet.'

Then he cut the frog's front legs off and ordered, 'Jump, frog, jump!'

The frog struggled and jumped.

The scientist noted in his journal, 'Frog with two legs jumped two feet.'

Next, the scientist cut off the frog's back legs. Once more, he shouted, 'Jump, frog, jump!'

The frog just lay there.

'Jump, frog, jump!' the scientist repeated.

Nothing.

The scientist noted in his journal, 'Frog with no legs is deaf.'

Hamster and Frogs

A down and out, grungy man walks into a swanky restaurant desperately needing a meal. He asks the waiter if he can have a free meal and the waiter says, 'Absolutely not! This is an upscale establishment and I'm going to have to ask you to leave.'

The man says, 'If I can show you something amazing that you've never seen before will you give me a meal?'

The waiter replies, 'OK, only if it is truly amazing and not crude.'

The man pulls a hamster out of his pocket. It jumps off the table, runs across the room to the piano and begins playing songs. And, it is really good!

The waiter is amazed and brings a hot meal to the man while the hamster plays.

When the man finishes, he is still hungry and asks the waiter for a free dessert and coffee.

The waiter says, 'No, sorry, unless you have money or another miracle, that's all you get.'

The man says, 'OK!' and pulls a frog out of his pocket and sets it on the table. The frog begins singing the song that the hamster is playing on the piano!

A man at another table rushes over and offers $200 for the singing frog. The man makes the trade and the fellow runs out of the restaurant with the frog to get him on the Tonight Show.

The waiter says, 'Are you crazy? That singing frog is worth millions, not just $200.'

The man replies, 'Not so. The hamster is also a ventriloquist. Now, bring that chocolate torte and coffee, please.'

Bear Attack

A Boy Scout hiking in Glacier Park recently was chased by a grizzly bear. He reached safety in a ranger station only to be arrested by park rangers. It seems it is illegal to run through the park with a bear behind.

Empire State Building

Two men are drinking in a bar at the top of the Empire State Building.

First says to the other, "I discovered last week that if you jump from the top of this building, the winds whipping around the skyscrapers will stop your fall and blow you right back up here."

"No way," replied the second man.

"Here, I'll prove it," said the first, and he jumped out the window. As he predicted, he fell a few feet and then returned right back through the window.

"Amazing!" exclaimed the second man, "Let me try that." He jumped, and fell all the way to the pavement below.

The bartender says to the first man, "You know, Superman, sometimes you're not very funny."

Letter from Camp

Dear Mom & Dad,

We are having a great time here at Camp Catcha Cough. Our Scoutmaster is making us all write to our parents in case you saw the flood on TV and worried. We are OK. Only 1 of our tents and 2 sleeping bags got washed away.

Luckily, none of us got drowned because we were all up on the mountain looking for Charlie when it happened. Oh yes, please call Charlie's mother and tell her he is OK. He can't write because of the cast. I got to ride in one of the search & rescue jeeps. It was neat. We never would have found him in the dark if it hadn't been for the lightning.

Scoutmaster got mad at Charlie for going on a hike alone without telling anyone. Charlie said he did tell him, but it was during the fire so he probably didn't hear him. Did you know that if you put gas on a fire, the gas could blow up? The wet wood still didn't burn, but one of our tents did. Also, some of our clothes. John is going to look weird until his hair grows back.

We will be home on Saturday if Scoutmaster gets the car fixed. It wasn't his fault about the wreck. The brakes worked OK when we left. Scoutmaster said that a car that old you have to expect something to break down; that's probably why he can't get insurance on it. We think it's a neat car. He doesn't care if we get it dirty, and if it's hot, sometimes he lets us ride on the tailgate. It gets pretty hot with 10 people in a car. He let us take turns riding in the trailer until the highway patrolman stopped and talked to us.

Our Scoutmaster is a neat guy. Don't worry, he is a good driver. In fact, he is teaching Travis how to drive. But he only lets him drive on the mountain roads where there isn't any traffic. All we ever see up there are logging trucks.

This morning all of the guys were diving off the rocks and swimming out in the lake. Scoutmaster wouldn't let me because I can't swim and Charlie was afraid he would sink because of his cast, so he let us take the canoe across the lake. It was great. You can still see some of the trees under the water from the flood. Scoutmaster isn't crabby like some scoutmasters. He didn't even get mad about the life jackets.

He has to spend a lot of time working on the car so we are trying not to cause him any trouble. Guess what? We have all passed our first aid merit badges. When David dove in the lake and cut his arm, we got to see how a tourniquet works. Also Raymond and I threw up. Scoutmaster said it probably was just food poisoning from the leftover chicken.

I have to go now. We are going into town to mail our letters and buy bullets. Don't worry about anything. We are fine.

Love,
Your son

P.S. How long has it been since I had a tetanus shot?

Lost Dog

Jim: Why are you crying?

Joe: My dog's lost.

Jim: Maybe he'll just come home.

Joe: No he won't, he's lost.

Jim: Well, I'll help you put Lost Dog posters up if you want.

Joe: Naw, it wouldn't do any good.

Jim: Why not?

Joe: My dog can't read!

Murphy's Law

Any stone in a hiking boot migrates to the location of maximum pressure.

Remaining distance to a given campsite remains constant as twilight approaches.

Number of mosquitoes at any given location is inversely proportional to the volume of remaining repellent.

The probability of finding a latrine is one over the number of poison ivy plants per acre.

The square feet of level ground available for tents equals the degrees from horizon of the setting sun.

The need to urinate at night increases in direct relation to the hour past midnight, layers of clothing worn, occupants in your tent, and inches of rain since sunset. Curiously, it increases in 'inverse' relation to the outside temperature.

The ground under shoulders compresses without sunlight while the ground under feet expands.

Rocks and sticks rise above dirt when irritated by tent flooring fabric.

Feet expand when removed from hiking boots. The same law applies to tents and tent bags, clothing and backpacks, and sleeping bags and stuff sacks.

Backpack strap widths decrease with the distance hiked. To compensate, the weight of the backpack increases.

Average local temperature increases with the amount of clothing packed.

Tent stakes come only in the quantity 'N-1' where N is the number of stakes necessary to stake down a tent.

Fuel in sealed bottles spontaneously evaporates.

Fuel in stove reservoirs evaporates 10x as fast as fuel in sealed bottles.

All available humidity and moisture will congregate on match heads.

If no match heads are in the vicinity, all moisture will congregate inside waterproof clothing.

The one new tent on the trip that leaks will be yours.

The side of the tent that leaks will be your side.

All food assumes a common taste and color when freeze-dried.

Divide the number of servings by two when reading the directions for reconstituting anything freeze-dried.

When reading the instructions of a pump-activated water filter, 'hour' should be substituted for 'minute' when reading the average quarts filtered per minute.

A backpack's weight load migrates up and back the longer it is in motion.

All tree branches in a forest grow outward from their respective trunks at exactly the height of your nose. If you are male, tree branches will also grow at groin height.

Swiss Army Knife toothpicks and tweezers evaporate open contact with air.

Rain happens.

Waterproof clothing isn't. (However, it is 100% effective at containing sweat).

Non-stick pans aren't.

Waterproof matches aren't.

One size fits all don't.

Anything bug-proof isn't.

A backpack's weight is not affected by the amount of food eaten out of it.

The minimum temperature rating for any sleeping bag raises as the external temperature lowers.

Ropes holding bear bags stretch.

The loudness of an animal at night grows as the size of the animal shrinks.

The sun sets 47% faster than normal when setting up camp. It sets another 28% faster if rain is eminent.

Of a 25% chance of rain, 100% will fall in your campsite.

When hiking, you take half as many downhill steps as uphill.

95% of a backpack's contents could have been left at home.

The 5% left at home will be needed.

The memory of misery approaches zero as the memory of joy approaches infinity.

Nasty Bug

Last week, I was watching a show on TV about invading space aliens - it was pretty creepy. Then, the doorbell rang so I went to answer it. Standing there was a 6-foot-tall mosquito! He grabbed me by the neck, threw me across the room, and then left.

The next night, I was playing a video game and the doorbell rang. I answered it and that same six-foot mosquito was there. He punched me in the stomach and then thumped me on the head and left.

The third night, the doorbell rang. I slowly opened the door and that mosquito pushed the door open, hit me in both eyes, kicked me in the shin, and body slammed me to the ground then left.

The next day, I went to see my doctor and explained everything that had happened. I asked him what I should do.

The doctor replied, "Not much you can do. There's just a nasty bug going around."

Pinewood Derby

Top ten signs that dad is taking the Pinewood Derby too seriously:
Dad 'trash talks' the tiger cubs

The Scout gets his first look at the car as he walks to the registration table

Dad keeps referring to it as 'my car'

Car and Driver magazine wants to feature your car on next month's cover

Dad threatens to break the Scout's fingers if he touches it after the wheels are on

Mom asks the Cubmaster to delay the start of the race because "we're still taking bets"

Dad asked Santa for a Pinewood Derby track for Christmas

"What? You mean there are no trophies for the adults?"

Even though he is in the stands, 60' feet away, dad is sure the finish line judge called it wrong

At the end of the race, Dad is the one crying

Silent Odorless Farts

An old man visited his doctor for help with a problem.

"Doc, I don't know what's wrong, but I fart all the time. It's weird because they are silent and odorless, but they keep coming out. In fact, I've farted about 6 times just sitting here. What can I do?"

The doctor replied, "Here, take one of these pills every morning and then come see me in a week."

A week later, the old man came back to the doctor and he was upset. "Doc, those pills didn't help - they made it worse! I'm still farting, but now they stink something fierce!"

The doctor replied, "Calm down, sir. Now that we've cleared your sinuses, we can work on your hearing."

Smoke Signals

First: Hey, look way off over there. What's that?
Second: Wow, smoke signals!
First: What do they say?
Second: Help ... my ... blankets ... on ... fire!

Starry Skies

The Scoutmaster and his Tenderfoot son went on a camping trip. As they lay down for the night, the Tenderfoot said, "Dad, look up into the sky and tell me what you see".

His Scoutmaster father responded, "I see millions and millions of stars".

Tenderfoot Son: "And what does that tell you?"

Scoutmaster Dad: "Astronomically, it tells me that there are millions of galaxies and potentially billions of planets. Theologically, it tells me that God is great and that we are small and insignificant. Meteorologically, it tells me that we will have a beautiful day tomorrow. What does it tell you, son?"

Tenderfoot Son: "It tells me you forgot to pack the tent again"

Build a Campfire Joke

- Split dead limb into fragments and shave one fragment into slivers.
- Bandage left thumb.
- Chop other fragments into smaller fragments.
- Bandage left foot.
- Make a structure of slivers (including those embedded in the hand).
- Light match.
- Light match.
- Repeat "A Scout is cheerful" and light match.
- Apply match to slivers, add wood fragments, and blow gently into base of flames.
- Apply burn ointment to nose.
- When fire is burning, collect more wood.
- When fire is burning well, add all remaining firewood.
- After thunderstorm has passed, repeat the above steps.

Survival Cards

The scoutmaster was teaching the scouts about survival in the desert.

"What are the three most important things you should bring with you in case you get lost in the desert?" he asked. Several hands went up, and many important things were suggested such as food, matches, etc.

Then one young scout raised his hand.

"Yes Johnny, what are the three most important things you would bring with you?" asked the Scoutmaster.

Johnny replied, "A compass, a canteen of water, and a deck of cards."

"Why's that Johnny?"

Johnny answered, "The compass is to find the right direction and the water is to prevent dehydration..."

"And what about the deck of cards?" asked the scoutmaster.

"Well, Sir, as soon as you start playing Solitaire, someone is bound to come up behind you and say, 'Put that red nine on top of that black ten!'"

Two Cannibals

Two cannibals are eating a clown. One says to the other: 'Does this taste funny to you?'

Watch for Bears

The National Park Rangers are advising hikers in Glacier National Park and other Rocky Mountain parks to be alert for bears and take extra precautions to avoid an encounter.

They advise park visitors to wear little bells on their clothes so they make noise when hiking. The bell noise allows bears to hear them coming from a distance and not be startled by a hiker accidentally sneaking up on them. This might cause a bear to charge.

Visitors should also carry a pepper spray can just in case a bear is encountered. Spraying the pepper into the air will irritate the bear's sensitive nose and it will run away.

It is also a good idea to keep an eye out for fresh bear scat so you have an idea if bears are in the area. People should be able to recognize the difference between black bear and grizzly bear scat.

Black bear droppings are smaller and often contain berries, leaves, and possibly bits of fur. Grizzly bear droppings tend to contain small bells and smell of pepper.

Bulls Wobble

A herd of cows and two bulls are eating grass out in the pasture.

Suddenly, a great gust of wind comes ripping across the prairie and knocks all the cows to the ground. But, the bulls just sway in the wind and continue eating.

When the wind quiets down, the cows stand up, brush off the dirt, and start eating again.

A bit later, one cow looks up just in time to see a tornado tearing through the pasture fence. The tornado knocks the cows every which way, but the bulls just rock back and forth as they are buffeted.

When the cows get back on their feet and pick the straw out of their hide, they all walk over to the bulls.

One cow says, "Why do we cows get knocked over by wind but you bulls keep standing?"

The two bulls laugh and reply, "We bulls wobble, but we don't fall down."

Where is God?

There were two young scouts that were twins and they did not quite get the Scout Oath. They stole things, swore, and generally got themselves into trouble around town when they were not on scout outings.

Their mother, realizing she needed help, asked the Scoutmaster to talk with them. He agreed and decided to see them one at a time and hopefully get them to understand that they needed to change. He thought he would first get them to see that their actions were sinful.

When the first scout arrived, he was sat in a chair and the Scoutmaster, who was a big man with a pretty loud voice asked, "Where is God?" He wanted to get the scout to understand that God is everywhere.

The scout's mouth dropped open, but he said nothing. So, the scoutmaster repeated more sternly, "Where is God?"

Again, the scout just sat and stared dumbly at the Scoutmaster so he raised his voice and asked a third time, "WHERE IS GOD?"

The little scout screamed, jumped up, ran out the door, all the way home, into his room, dove into his closet, and hid under his dirty clothes. And, that's where his brother found him.

He asked, "What happened?"

The first scout replied, "Man, we are in BIG trouble! God is missing and they think WE took him!"

Chicken Crossing the Road

Why Did the Chicken Cross the Road?

Shrek: Urrrrrp - What chicken?
George Bush: To face a kinder, gentler thousand points of headlights
Darwin: It was the logical next step after coming down from the trees
Bob Dylan: How many roads must one chicken cross?
Robert Frost: To cross the road less traveled by
Gilligan: The traffic started getting rough; the chicken had to cross. If not for the plumage of its peerless tail the chicken would be lost, the chicken would be lost!
Martin Luther King: It had a dream
James T. Kirk: To boldly go where no chicken has gone before
Sir Isaac Newton: Chickens at rest tend to stay at rest. Chickens in motion tend to cross the road
Mr. Scott: 'Cos ma wee transporter beam was na functioning properly. Ah canna work miracles, Captain!
Mae West: I invited it to come up and see me sometime
George Washington: Actually it crossed the Delaware with me back in 1776

Albert Einstein: Whether the chicken crossed the road or the road crossed the chicken depends upon your frame of reference
Darth Vader: Because it could not resist the power of the Dark Side
Lord Baden-Powell: To earn a Road Crossing merit badge
Colonel Sanders: I missed one?

Irish Farmer

An old Irish farmer's dog goes missing and he's inconsolable
His wife says: "Why don't you put an ad in the paper?"
The farmer does. Two weeks later the dog is still missing.
"What did you put in the paper?" his wife asks.
"Here boy" he replies.

3 Guys

3 guys were walking along a beach and came across an old lamp. One of them rubbed the lamp and a genie popped out. He said they could each have a wish. The first guy said he wanted to be 10 times smarter. Your wish is granted, said the genie. The second, said I want to be 100 times smarter. Your wish is granted! The third guy wished to be 1000 times smarter. The genie asked if he was certain that was his wish. The guy said yes and bam, he was a woman!

Canada

An elderly woman lived on a small farm in Canada, just yards away from the North Dakota border. Their land had been the subject of a minor dispute between the United States and Canada for years. The now widowed woman lived on the farm with her son and three grandchildren. One day her son came into her room holding a letter.

"I just got some news, Mom," he said. "The government has come to an agreement with the people in North Dakota. They've decided that our land is really part of the United States. We have the right to approve or disapprove of the agreement. What do you think?"

"What do I think?" his mother said. "Sign it! Call them right now and tell them we accept! I don't think I could stand another one of those Canadian winters!"

Father and Son

Father: Which one do you love more , me or Mommy?
Son: I love you both.
Father: Very Well , lets say I went to Japan and Mommy went to France which country will you go to?
Son: Japan.

Father: See, that you love Mommy more than me?

Son: No, I just want to visit Japan.

Father: Very well , lets say I went to Japan and Mommy went to France which country will you go to?

Son: France.

Father: See?

Son: No its just because I have already visited Japan.

Graveyard

Francesca went to the cemetery in her village to water the flowers on the grave of her deceased husband Enzo.

When she was finished, she always walked backwards when she left the grave site.

One day her friend, Bianca asked, "Francesca, why do you always leave the cemetery walking backwards?"

Francesca answered, "When Enzo was alive he always told me, 'You've got such a great butt it could bring a dead man back to life. So, I'm not taking any chances!!'"

You are Taking Scouting Too Seriously If...

- You buy that '89 Chevy Caprice because you really like that fleur de lis hood ornament
- Your favorite color is "olive drab"
- You decide to lash together the new deck on the back of your house
- You plan to serve foil meals at your next dinner party
- You walk the streets in broad daylight with a coffee cup and flashlight hanging from your belt
- You raise your hand in the scout sign at a heated business meeting
- You were arrested by airport security because you wouldn't give up your official Boy Scout pocket knife until the officer said "thank you"
- You didn't mind losing power to your house for three days
- Your son hides his copy of Leader Magazine from you
- Your plans for remodeling the bathroom include digging the hole deeper
- You trade your 25-foot center console fishing boat in on that great little 15-foot canoe
- Your favorite movie is "Follow Me Boys" staring Fred MacMurry, and you spent months trying to convince Disney to release it on home video
- You managed to find that 8th day in the week
- You disconnect the automatic dishwasher in favor of the "3 pot method"
- You sneak a cup of "bug juice" after the troop turns in for the night

- You can start a fire by rubbing two sticks together
- Latrines at camp start becoming comfortable
- You think campaign hats are cool
- You gave your wife a mummy bag rated for -15 deg F for Christmas
- You name one of your kids Baden
- Your favorite tune is "Camp Granada"
- You can recite the Cub Law and Promise backwards, in order, in 3 seconds flat
- You bought 10,000 shares of Coleman stock on an inside tip they were about to release a microwave accessory for their camp stove line
- You can't eat eggs anymore unless they are cooked in a zip-lock bag
- You plan to get rich by writing a best-selling Dutch Oven cook book
- You took a chemistry course at the local college to help you develop a better fire starter
- You actually own a left-handed smoke shifter
- The height of your social season is the district recognition dinner
- You were disappointed when Leader magazine didn't win the Pulitzer Prize last year
- The Scouts in your troop chipped in to have you abducted by a professional cult de-programmer.

~ RIDDLES ~

WHO WILL BE FIRST TO GET THE ANSWER?

A woman is travelling around London when she passes Trafalgar Square she is sent straight to jail but she has done nothing wrong. Why is this?
Answer) She is playing monopoly.

Forwards I am heavy, backwards I am not. What am I?
Answer) Weight.

Brothers and sisters I have none but this man's father is my father's son. Who is the man?
Answer) The man is my son

A cowboy rides into town on Friday he spends two nights there. Then leaves on Friday. How is this possible?
Answer) His horse is called Friday.

Two fathers and two sons go fishing they each catch a fish and return with three fish only why?
Answer) There was a grandfather a father and a son.

A man is travelling towards the center of a field; he knows that when he gets there he is going to be badly injured. Why does he know this?
Answer) He has jumped from an airplane and his parachute has failed to open.

A man lives on the 20th floor of a block of flats every night when he returns home he takes the lift up 10 floors and walks the rest of the way but in the morning he takes the lift from the 20th floor to the ground floor. Why does he do this?
Answer) The man is very short and cannot reach the button that takes him to the 20th floor.

There are twenty sick sheep grazing in a field, overnight three sheep sadly die leaving 17 sheep. How is this possible?
Answer) 20 sick will be heard as 26.

A man is stuck inside a concrete dome; the dome has no windows and no doors. All he has is a cake and a penknife. How does he escape?
Answer) He cuts the cake in to halves. Two halves make a hole and he crawls out though the hole.

Each morning I appear to lie at your feet. All day I will follow you no matter how fast you run. Yet I nearly perish in the midday sun.
Answer) Shadow

You can see nothing else when you look in my face. I'll look you in the eye but will never lie.
Answer) Reflection

At the sound of me, men may dream or stamp their feet. At the sound of me, women may laugh or sometimes weep
Answer) Music

Until I am measured I am not known, yet how you miss me when I have flown away.
Answer) Time

What occurs once in a minute, twice in a moment but never in an hour?
Answer) The letter 'm'

I go up and down stairs without moving.
Answer) A carpet

Give it food and it will live.
Answer) Fire

What Am I

If you want to camp outdoors
This will protect you from the rain
It is held up by some poles
A sleeping bag it does contain
If you like being round nature
And overnight want to camp
You might sleep inside one of these
To stop you from getting damp
Answer) Tent

What Am I

I am a type of mammal
Whose height and strength are very great
I have big paws and thick fur
And in dark caves I hibernate
What is this type of animal?
A cartoon had one called Yogi
Then there's the well-known Paddington
And in The Muppets there's Fozzie
If you see one when you're camping
It might give you a big fright

They can be black, brown or grizzly
And pandas are black and white
What is this type of animal?
The Jungle Book had Baloo
Smokey warns you about fires
There's also Winnie-The-Pooh
Answer) Bear

What Am I

If you're sailing on a pirate ship
To find your way you'll need at least this item that will help guide the way
By pointing north, south, west and east
You can navigate by the sun and stars
But there's another way that's the best
An item that uses magnetic fields
To point which way is north, south, east and west
If you're lost in the middle of nowhere
Then firstly make sure your eyes are peeled
And hope your backpack contains this item
That guides using the Earth's magnetic field
If you get lost somewhere
There's no need to raise a rumpus
First of all, just stay calm
And pull out your trusty...
Answer) Compass

Short Riddles

Why is the little ant always confused?
Because all his uncles are ants.

What is the best part of a Boxer's joke?
The PUNCH line.

What kind of house weighs the least?
A LIGHT house.

Why is a river rich?
It has two banks.

How many seconds are there in a year?
A: 12 - Jan. 2, Feb. 2, Mar. 2, ...

Who sleeps with their shoes on?
Horses.

Prove that a cat has 3 tails.
No cat has 2 tails and one cat has one more tail than no cat, so one cat has 3 tails.

What is faster - heat or cold?
Heat - you can catch cold.

A farmer had 17 sheep. All but 9 died. How many does he have now?
Nine.

Take 2 apples from 3 apples and what do you have?
2 apples.

What word in the dictionary is always spelled wrong?
WRONG.

What question can you never truthfully answer 'Yes'?
Are you asleep?

Which is the quietest sport?
Bowling - you can hear a pin drop.
What occurs once in a minute, twice in a moment, but never in an hour?
The letter M.

What goes around the world but stays in a corner?
A postage stamp.

What kind of room has no door or windows?
A mushroom.

What word starts with an 'E' and has only one letter in it?
An Envelope.

Why did the Texan buy a dachshund?
Because all the other cowboys were saying, 'Get a-long little doggie!'

What does a horse say when he's finished eating his hay?
Well, that's the last straw!

Why do cowboys always die with their boots on?

So they won't stub their toes when they kick the bucket!

How do you find a lost rabbit?
Make a noise like a carrot.

What food can never become the heavyweight champion of the world?
The lollipop. It always gets licked!

What do you call a cat who eats a lemon?
A sourpuss!

Where do most outstanding hamburgers end up?
In the Hall of Flame!

What did the hamburger say to the pickle?
You're dill-icious!

What do you call a blind dinosaur?
Do-you-think-he-saur-us.

What do you call a blind dinosaur's dog?
Do-you-think-he-saur-us-Rex.

Where do you find an ocean with no water?
On a map.

What gets bigger the more you take away?
A hole.

What can you catch but never throw?
A cold.

What word becomes shorter when you add two letters to it?
Short.

What has hands but can not clap?
A clock.

What stays where it is when it goes off?
An alarm clock.

What goes up and doesn't come back down? – Your age.

What gets wetter as it dries?
A towel.

What belongs to you but is used more by others?
Your name.

I'm full of keys but I can't open any doors. What am I?
A piano.

What comes once in a minute, twice in a moment and never in a thousand years?
The letter M.

Which word in the dictionary is spelled incorrectly?
Incorrectly.

What is always coming but never arrives?
Tomorrow.

What tastes better than it smells?
A tongue.

~ FUNNY STORIES ~

KIDS CURL UP IN A CHAIR AND DO SOME READING

JUST A HIKE IN THE WOODS

A guy's going on a hiking vacation through the mountains Out West. Before setting off into the boonies, he stops into a small general store to get some supplies.

After picking out the rest of his provisions, he asks the old store owner, "Say, Mister, I'm going hiking up in the mountains, and I was wondering; do you have any bears around here?"

"Yup," replies the owner.

"What kind?" asks the hiker.

"Well, we got black bears and we got grizzlies," he replies.

"I see," says the hiker. "Do you have any of those bear bells?"

"What do you mean?" asks the store owner.

"You know," replies the hiker, "those little tinkle-bells that people wear in bear country to warn the bears that they are coming, so they don't surprise the bears and get attacked."

"Oh yeah," replies the owner. "They're over there," he says, pointing to a shelf on the other side of the store. The hiker selects a couple of the bells and takes them to the counter to pay for them.

"Tell me something, Mister," the hiker inquires, "how can you tell when you're in bear territory, anyway?"

"By the scat," the old fellow replies, ringing up the hiker's purchases.

"Well, um, how can I tell if it's grizzly territory or black bear territory?" the hiker asks.

"By the scat," the store owner replies.

"Well, what's the difference?" asks the hiker. "I mean, what's different between grizzly scat and black bear scat?"

"The stuff that's in it," replies the store owner.

Getting a little frustrated, the hiker asks, "OK, so what's in grizzly bear scat that isn't in black bear scat?" he asks, an impatient tone in his voice.

Bear bells, replies the old man as he hands the hiker his purchases.

ON THE TRAIN

A young boy was traveling on a long train trip across Canada. Sitting across from him was an older man, very neatly and precisely dressed. Across his knees he carried a briefcase upon which he nervously drummed his fingers. Since he looked to be rather an angry sort of man, the boy didn't want to start a conversation.

Presently the man opened the briefcase and took out two paper napkins, a pocketknife and an apple. Carefully he peeled and cored the apple. He placed all the peelings on one of the two napkins and folded it into a neat parcel. Then he moved his briefcase to one side, stood up, and walked to the end of the coach. By craning his neck, the boy was able to watch him move out onto the little platform at the end of the car and throw the parcel of peel onto the tracks.

When the man returned he dusted his hands, sat down and lifted the briefcase back up across his knees. He picked up the peeled and cored apple, carefully cut it into thin slices, placed the slices onto the second napkin and made a similar neat parcel. To the boy's amazement he then repeated his routine. He moved to the end of the coach and threw the parcel on the line. When he returned, he picked up his briefcase, took out two more napkins and an orange which he began to peel...

(Now you spin out the story, having the man take all kinds of fruit, one at a time, from his case, peel each piece and throw away first the peel and then the fruit itself)

At last the young boy could contain himself no longer and simply had to ask the man what he was doing.

"I'm making a fruit salad," said the man.

"Then why do you keep throwing it away?" the boy asked."

"I should think that was obvious," snapped the man. "I'm throwing it away because I don't like fruit salad!"

RABBI LIEBNER IN THE VALLEY OF THREADS

On the topic of celestial guidance, Rabbi Liebner has something of an odd contribution...

The town of Treadville was small but prosperous and lay in a high valley surrounded by higher mountains. The Treads (for that is what they named themselves) were wealthy enough to love more than work and humble enough to make more than money. Little disturbed their peace until a late autumn night.

On that night, the Treads beheld a small but bright light gleaming from the top of a neighboring mountain. Curious in their ease, they soon decided to climb the mountain -- the highest of those around -- to discover the source of the light.

None arrived at the summit. At a point about halfway to the peak an extension of the mountain, seem less in the granite and shaped like an immense foot, lurched from the slope and hurled the luckless climbers from the slope. Strangely, few were harmed by the fall, but none reached the peak.

And so for years, decades, and then centuries the Treads wondered what could be the source of that radiant glow? Then, one day, one Rabbi Liebner entered the village and learned of the mystery of Tread Valley. The Rabbi was fascinated by the story and felt the touch of God in its weave. That night he watched the light and knew. He knew that he had been chosen to seek its source.

The Treads were not jealous of their mysteries; they invited the Rabbi to climb the peak the next day... and made all preparations for his inevitable fall. Thus, he set out.

That afternoon, Rabbi Liebner reached Foot's Fall, the point where the mountain made its wishes known.... and nothing happened. The Rabbi continued upwards to the cheers of the town; at sunset he reached the summit.

There, on the mountain's brow, he stumbled to a halt. Before him stood a brilliant temple bathed in celestial light, encircled be a holy sheen. Rabbi Liebner was awed. Finally, he summoned the strength to murmur a question and a prayer. "Oh Lord, thank you for this vision! But why have I been chosen to surmount this peak? Why not the good people of Treadville in the many years they have tried?"

And to his eternal joy, the Rabbi heard in a thunderous voice from heaven, "Silly Rabbi, kicks are for Treads."

A LONG WAY TO GO

It came to pass that a very poor peasant was down to his last meal.

Deciding he could no longer live in squalor, he decide to sell the only thing he owned... his talking mule. These was no ordinary type of talking mule, this one could tell jokes and sing and keep the local townspeople very happy. With much regret, the peasant sets off to the big city to sell his mule.

He sets up on a street corner and the mule draws an immediate crowd. The mule is so funny that the crowds can't remain standing because they're laughing so hard. Finally, a man comes up to the peasant and says "I'm a talent scout for The Tonight Show. I MUST have your mule for our show." Unfortunately, the talent scout had just been pick pocketed, and had lost his wallet. The only thing of value he had was a subway token. He convinced the peasant to trade the mule for the "Magic Token of Good Fortune" and secured the mule.

On the way home, the peasant realized that he had been cheated, and he was broken hearted. He used his subway token to get him to the edge of the city. When he put the token in the slot, alarms went off and he was notified that he was the 1 billionth rider of the subway, and that he just won 50 million dollars.

Meanwhile, the Mule was so funny that he took over Jay's job, and eventually put Dave, Conan, John and every other late nighter out of business. The Morale of the story: A Mule that is funny is soon bartered.

DANCES WITH CUCUMBERS

May 5, 1863 -- Here on the frontier, I sometimes wonder if the ancients were right. With no other friendly face within 150 miles, it seems as if I _have_ fallen off the edge of the Earth.

I spend my time now reading what books I have and cultivating my patch of cucumbers (which I brought back from the Holy Land, cf. _Prince_of_Thieves_). The "purpose" of this fort, to hold back the Indians, has fallen away with my civilized veneer.

May 7, 1863 -- This morning I had an interesting and silent encounter. One of the tribe of Indians nearby watched me perform my morning tasks and then left without a word. I am excited by the prospect of contact with the natives of the area.

May 20, 1863 -- I have finally convinced the Indians to parlay with me. I taught them the word for "fort", feeling that it would be simple enough for them to learn. They in turn taught me the Indian word "titonka", apparently a small but tough, powerfully merchandised horseless carriage of metal construction. I envy these people their simplicity.

June 7, 1863 -- Today I visited the Indians' village. It is on one of the many flat-topped plateaus in the area. As the decline of the buffalo proceeds, so too does this Indian tribe face decline. I will try to teach them agriculture. They have also told me their name for themselves. It is "Anasazi"... which apparently means "people called Anasazi" in their language. I am called by them "Stinchapecsal" which means "he who should bathe more regularly".

July 8, 1863 -- A rude awakening. The Indians are fully aware of agriculture and in fact have nothing to do with the buffalo (what kind of nomadic tribe would build a village on a _mesa_?); unfortunately, they are suffering a drought.

Knowing a remedy, I have told them to dig a ditch from the nearby stream up the mountainside to their mesa-top fields. In the meantime, I am pickling my cucumbers.

July 20, 1863 -- The drought is desperate, but the ditch is finished and my pickles are ready. I am lining the ditch with pickles. The Anasazi are doubtful, but I have promised them results in the morning.

July 21, 1863 -- Success! The stream has been diverted and now flows up the mountainside to the Anasazi fields. Amazed by this seeming magic, I told them that it was simply a well-known fact in my world. After all, everyone knows that "dill waters run steep".

DOGS IN THE WILD WEST

One hot and dry day in the Wild West, this dog walks into a saloon and says, "Gimme a beer". Evidently this type of thing wasn't too rare 'round those parts because the bartender said, "I'm sorry, but we don't serve dogs here." The dog then took out a silver dollar, dropped it on the bar, and said, "Look, I got money, and I want a beer." This scene had the potential to get ugly. The bartender, getting a little irate, said one more time, "We do not serve dogs here. Please leave." The dog growled, so the bartender pulled out a gun and shot the dog in the foot! The dog yelped, and ran out the door.

The next day, the swinging bar doors were tossed open and in walks the dog that had been in the saloon the day before. He was dressed all in black. A black cowboy hat, a black vest, three black cowboy boots and one black bandage. The dog looks around, waits for the talking to quiet down, and says, "I'm lookin' fer the man who shot my paw."

SNEAKERS

Only his mother and father called him Todd. To every Scout in Eagle District the name Todd suggested just one nickname, "TOAD", which Toad didn't mind at all. You see, Toad wanted, more than anything else in the world to win the smelly-sneaker contest.

Toad's sneakers were smelly. No doubt of that. But the first year he entered the Indian Nations Council Great Smelly Sneaker Contest, he didn't even get third prize.

The second year Toad entered the smelly-sneaker contest, he worked hard at it all year. He had already learned from an Eagle Scout that not wearing sox mattered. By not wearing sox, Toad made his sneakers much, much smellier. In addition, Toad fudged on his showers. He turned on the water. He more or less got into the shower and more or less washed most of himself, including his hair. He knew his mom and dad could tell the difference between the smell of clean hair and the smell of dirty hair, but they trusted him to wash his feet. Toad did not wash his feet, which helped the smell of his sneakers considerably.

Still, that second year Toad got only second place.

Toad was bitterly disappointed. After the contest, he stood sad and dejected by a large garbage can, trying to decide if he should just chuck those second-place sneakers right into the garbage.

"Hey kid!" called a hoarse voice from the other side of the can.

"Hey, kid!!!!" the voice insisted.

"Yeah?" said Toad.

"How much you wanna win that contest?"

"More than anything!" said Toad.

"I know how you can win, " the voice said.

Toad peered around the garbage can, where a big skinny kid sat on the ground.

"What'll ya give me if I tell?"

Without hesitation, Toad offered his brand new back pack, the thing he loved most, the one he'd worked all summer to earn the money for. He'd give the back pack. Toad offered it to the kid sitting beside the garbage can.

"Here's what ya do," said the kid, and he whispered instructions into Toad's ear, then he put a small vial into Toad's hand.

"Thanks" said Toad.

The kid stood up, shrugged.

With a smile of pure delight, Toad offered the tall skinny kid his back pack, but the kid turned his back. "Awww....Keep it," was all he said.

Toad raced home. The contest rules said you had to start the year with a clean pair of sneakers. Some Scouts tried to cheat, but not Toad. He was sure he'd win, for in the vial was essence of sneaker, foot sweat mixed with scrapings from the sneakers of the last four winners of the Indian Nations Council Great Smelly Sneaker Contest grand prize. Toad put the precious droplets into his new sneakers. The results were instant and made Toad's eyes water.

All that year he went sockless and put plastic bags on his sneakers at night to keep the smell in, even though his parents made him put the sneakers outside. After a few days, at the next troop meeting, even his Scout Master, insisted that Toad's sneakers be left outside. Toad did as his Scout Master said, first bagging the sneakers to keep the concentrated smell from getting diluted.

Toad's dedication and hard work paid off. As the day of the Indian Nations Council Great Smelly Sneaker Contest drew closer, it was clear to all of the Scouts that Toad would be the winner.

The first judge, a new, young assistant scout master, approached Toad's sneakers. From more than a yard away, he began to retch.

The Second judge, an old, experienced Scout Master, wiped his eyes, waved a group of papers before his face, and backed away from Toad's sneakers.

The Third judge, the District Executive took a whiff, grinned and said, "Now that's more like it!" and awarded Toad First Prize!

Toad was giddy with bliss. When the judges asked if he'd like to donate the sneakers to the Scouting Museum, Toad said "no". He'd wear them home. He'd savor being champion.

Off Toad went, right foot, left foot, wearing championship sneakers, ones you could smell from afar. Right foot, left foot.

Toad was a good long way from home when his left foot started to itch something awful right around his toes, but Toad did not stop to scratch. He went on and on, but Toad kept on walking.

And he walked and he walked, and the itch got to itching the whole sole of his right foot and then the whole sole of his left foot.

But Toad kept on walking, without stopping to scratch until he got home. And the itching was terrible-clear up to his ankles!

With a sigh of relief, Toad got home and reached down to take off his championship smelly sneakers.

But when Toad took of the Championship Smelly Sneakers and got ready to   scratch,   Toad   discovered   that.............
HIS
FEET
WERE
GONE!

THE BRONZE RAT

A tourist wanders into a back-alley antique shop in San Francisco's Chinatown. Picking through the objects on display he discovers a detailed, life-sized bronze sculpture of a rat. The sculpture is so interesting and unique that he picks it up and asks the shop owner what it costs.

"Twelve dollars for the rat, sir," says the shop owner, "and a thousand dollars more for the story behind it."

"You can keep the story, old man," he replies, "but I'll take the rat."

The transaction complete, the tourist leaves the store with the bronze rat under his arm. As he crosses the street in front of the store, two live rats emerge from a sewer drain and fall into step behind him. Nervously looking over his shoulder, he begins to walk faster, but every time he passes another sewer drain, more rats come out and follow him. By the time he's walked two blocks, at least a hundred rats are at his heels, and people begin to point and shout. He walks even faster, and soon breaks into a trot as multitudes of rats swarm from sewers, basements, vacant lots, and abandoned cars. Rats by the thousands are at his heels, and as he sees the waterfront at the bottom of the hill, he panics and starts to run full tilt.

No matter how fast he runs, the rats keep up, squealing hideously, now not just thousands but millions, so that by the time he comes rushing up to the water's edge a trail of rats twelve city blocks long is behind him. Making a mighty leap, he jumps up onto a light post, grasping it with one arm while he hurls the bronze rat into San Francisco Bay with the other, as far as he can heave it. Pulling his legs up and clinging to the light post, he watches in amazement as the seething tide of rats surges over the breakwater into the sea, where they drown.

Shaken and mumbling, he makes his way back to the antique shop.

"Ah, so you've come back for the rest of the story," says the owner.

No, says the tourist, I was wondering if you have a bronze lawyer.

THE CHICKEN IN THE LIBRARY

A librarian is working away at her desk when she notices that a chicken has come into the library and is patiently waiting in front of the desk. When the chicken sees that it has the librarian's attention, it squawks, "Book, book, book, BOOK!"

The librarian complies, putting a couple of books down in front of the chicken. The chicken quickly grabs them and disappears.

The next day, the librarian is again disturbed by the same chicken, who puts the previous day's pile of books down on the desk and again squawks, "Book, book, book, BOOK!"

The librarian shakes her head, wondering what the chicken is doing with these books, but eventually finds some more books for the chicken. The chicken disappears.

The next day, the librarian is once again disturbed by the chicken, who squawks (in a rather irritated fashion, it seems), "Book, book, book, BOOK!" By now, the librarian's curiosity has gotten the better of her, so she gets a pile of books for the chicken, and follows the bird when it leaves the library. She follows it through the parking lot, down the street for several blocks, and finally into a large park. The chicken disappears into a small grove of trees, and the librarian follows. On the other side of the trees is a small marsh. The chicken has stopped on the side of the marsh. The librarian, now really curious, hurries over and sees that there is a small frog next to the chicken, examining each book, one at a time. The librarian comes within earshot just in time to hear the frog saying, "Read it, read it, read it..."

THE DOCTOR

A doctor was just starting out on his own, when he found that he just had too much work to do. Now this man was brilliant, and had particularly good people skills. Once he got a patient, they would just not see anyone else.

It seems that this man had been reading recently about the advances in cloning, and decided to have a clone made of himself to do his work.

For years it worked perfectly. His clone took care of all his patients, and he got to relax. However, the clone began to have some personality disorders. It would insult patients, and treat them very badly. It got so bad that business was suffering. The doctor decided that he just had to get rid of the clone or lose his business.

So.....one morning on their morning jog.... they jogged right over a bridge. The doctor pushed the clone over to his death.

The doctor again began seeing his old patients, and things were going exceptionally well, until a fisherman "caught" the dead clone body in the river. When the police found that the real doctor was still, in fact, alive, and that this was a clone, they didn't know just what to charge the doctor for doing wrong. After much deliberation, they decided to charge him for... Making an obscene clone fall.

THE BANK ROBBER

The financial situation had been very bad for several months. Because he was out of work and destitute, a young man decided to rob a bank. After days of observation, he chose a small satellite bank facility across the metropolitan area from where he was living. He spent several days planning every move. Late one dark moonless night he picked the lock on the rear door of the bank without difficulty.

He stealthily crept through the bank to the place where he knew the safe stood. Then his troubles began. While trying to pick the lock on the safe, he set off the burglar alarm, but his careful preparation paid off. He had brought along a furniture dolly. He quickly loaded the small safe onto the dolly and rolled it out to his van.

He drove to a friend's house and explained his problem. He asked if, in exchange for some of the loot, he might store the safe in the friend's garage for a few days. His friend assured him: "You can rest assured, your safe is secret with me!"

SIR LANCELOT'S MISSION

King Arthur sends Sir Lancelot out on an important mission to deliver a message to the king of Spain. It is a long distance, and Lancelot looks in the Kingdom for a good horse to take him there. His own horse is sick, and all he can find is an old mare, but, since he has to leave quickly, he takes the mare.

About 3 days out of the Kingdom, Lancelot realizes his mistake. The horse gets tired and appears to be going lame. He finally makes it to a small village and gets to the Inn. He goes up to the Innkeeper and explains his problem. That is, he needs a good horse so that he can fulfill his mission to deliver the message for the king. The Innkeeper replies that this is only a small village, and most of the horses around are not up to the task. He is welcome to look around, however, and if he can find anything, he is certainly welcome to it.

Lancelot looks around the village, and true as the Innkeeper has said, no good horse is to be found. As Lancelot is about to give up, he comes across a stable boy carting some feed. He asks the stable boy if there is any beast of burden in the village that he can use to fulfill his mission. The stable boy thinks for a minute, and starts to reply no, but then says, go see if Old Mange in the barn can help you.

Lancelot goes over to the barn expecting to find a horse. What he finds is a very large dog: almost as large as a pony. The dog is a mess, however. It is mangy, parts of its fur are falling off, and it is full of fleas. Lancelot is desperate at this point, and he looks it over carefully. It does, however, appear to be strong enough to take him to Spain (which is only 3 days away at this point).

Lancelot goes back to the Innkeeper, and acknowledges that he cannot find a horse in the village that he can use. He says, however that this dog, Old Mange, might be able to take him most (if not all) of the way to his destination. The Innkeeper hears this, stiffens up, and says: Sir. I wouldn't send a Knight out on a dog like that.

STEP DRAG

IT WAS the hottest summer anyone could remember at Camp. It was between sessions and that meant the staff was left there all alone for a peaceful weekend.

Unknown to them, another bus - a gray prison bus - was winding along the road outside of the camp, transporting a single prisoner. The man was criminally insane, according to the tag on his prison uniform, and the two guards assigned to him believed it. He was very tall and strong, so his hands were manacled in huge handcuffs and his legs were hobbled close to each other with a chain. To keep him from running or kicking out at anyone, the Warden had added an old-fashioned ball and chain, which he'd found in a prison storeroom. That kind of thing hadn't been used since the 1920's. The chain was clamped to the maniac's right ankle, and the heavy iron ball was on the end of the four-foot chain.

The maniac was sitting quietly with his eyes closed, smiling that same simple smile he always smiled just to keep the guards wondering. Thinking that the maniac was asleep, the guards weren't being watchful enough. As the bus swerved on a tight mountain curve, one guard slid off the wooden bench and fell against the prisoner, who wasn't asleep at all. He quickly grabbed the guard by the neck with the short chain on his handcuffs.

While they struggled, the other guard got up and went after the maniac. The prisoner dropped the strangled guard and lunged at the other one. The guard tried to draw his pistol, but the maniac had picked up the iron ball and thrown it before the guard had so much as a chance.

The maniac found keys on the guard to remove the cuffs and the leg irons, but he could not find a key for the ball and chain. He picked up the iron ball again, smashed the wire glass window to the cab of the prison bus, and grabbed the driver by the throat. The bus swerved all over the road and finally crashed into the deep ditch beside the road, coming to rest against a large tree. The maniac was out!

Back at the Camp, the Staff had swum all afternoon and were now back in their tents on staff row, reading or listening to the radio. There wasn't a TV anywhere in the camp. The sun went down and the owls began to hoot scarily off in the distance. Suddenly someone screamed! Everyone came running out of their tents and met at the assembly ground.

Missy the swimming instructor was missing! The other four ran to her tent. The zipper was open and there was a pool of blood on the floor. The Staff gasped, then suddenly became very quiet.

"Ssshhh! Whispered David. They all strained to listen. In the trees, somewhere nearby they could hear:

Step... Drag... step ... drag... step ... drag...

"Let split up and look for her!" said Tim. They all ran off in different directions into the dark woods. After a few minutes David yelled for everyone to come to him. It was hard to follow his voice in the underbrush; it was hard to believe that the woods in camp were so thick and impenetrable. Soon Tim and Chris found David staring up into a tree. There in the moonlight was Colin. He was hanging by his head in a fork of the tree branches; his neck must have broken.

Off to the south they could hear noises in the under-growth: Step... Drag... step ... drag... step ... drag...

Tim climbed the tree and lowered the body to the others. The three of them carried the limp corpse back to the mess hall. Once inside, Tim hurried to lock all the doors with big wooden boards. "You all stay here", he said, "and lock this door behind me. I've got to get to the office where the phone is."

The others objected, but Tim went out the front door and slipped off in the darkness. The others dropped the wooden bar back into its metal brackets, to prevent anyone from entering. After a few minutes the lights suddenly went out. The staff started to scream, but then they realized that whoever had cut the wires might not know where they were. The held their hands over their mouths and hid under the serving counter.

Suddenly, something rattled the front door. It must be the maniac! The Staff huddled together. Next they heard something outside the window just above them, something dragging along the ground, going: Step... Drag... step ... drag... step ... drag...

The double doors rattled again. Tim whispered, "Hey dudes, let me in!" The dragging sound was moving around the building going toward the back door. Tim gasped louder, "Let me in!"

David ran from the Counter to the door and lifted the bar. Tim darted into the mess hall like a scared cat.

Just as they got the double doors shut, the dragging sound came around to the front. Just as they dropped the wooden bar into its brackets, something huge and heavy hit the door, cracking the wood.

Tim and Chris ran across the room, tripping and stumbling over chairs in the dark. The object hit the door again, and the wooden bar cracked with a loud noise. The two staffers looked under the serving counter. David wasn't there! They ran to the back door.

"The phone lines must have been cut whispered Tim. "The phone was dead". The heavy weight hit the front door again, breaking part of the doors upper half. Tim and Chris lifted the bar from the back door and swung it open. Another crash at the front door told then the doors were about to give. The two slipped into the tall pantry and closed the door.

Back in the mess hall, the double front doors gave way in a burst of splinters and broken boards. A deathly silence followed. The two staffers hardly dared to take a breath. Suddenly, they heard that sound out on the wooded floor: Step... Drag... step ... drag... step ... drag...

The sound stopped right outside the pantry door. Chris gasped. Tim cupped his hand over his mouth and the two held their breath. Tim was afraid the thing outside could hear his heart beating.

Suddenly there was a terrible scream outside the pantry.

It was David! He had moved to another hiding place, leaving Tim and Chris on their own. Now the thing, whatever it was had found him. There was another scream and the sound of something going out the back door.

Then everything was quiet as a graveyard.

The two waited all night, hardly breathing. The sun began to come up; they could see light coming in through the cracks of the wooden pantry. A morning dove was calling softly in the woods.

Then they heard a sound. Someone was coming in the front door. Slow footsteps crossed the floor, along with the sound of something dragging along the boards. The sound came closer to the pantry.

Suddenly it stopped, right in front of the pantry door as if someone was waiting.

Chris could not stand it anymore. He screamed.

The Pantry door swung open, and there standing over them was a tall, muscular form, lit from behind. The man bent over.

He took off his wide-brimmed hat and shows them his badge. "I'm the Sheriff", he said, dropping the heavy bag of weapons and bulletproof vest he had been dragging. "THANK GOD YOU TWO ARE ALL RIGHT!"

ANTI-BORING LIFESTYLE

WWW.SLOWSPRINT.COM

Made in the USA
Columbia, SC
10 April 2021

35928836R00098